Richard Wagner
Götterdämmerung

Richard Wagner
Götterdämmerung

translation and commentary
by Rudolph Sabor

For Hilde and Maurice

Phaidon Press Limited
Regent's Wharf
All Saints Street
London N1 9PA

First published 1997
© 1997 Phaidon Press Limited

ISBN 0 7148 3654 0

A CIP catalogue record for this
book is available from the
British Library

Printed in Hong Kong

Frontispiece, Brünnhilde with
the body of Siegfried; illustration
by Ludwig Burger (1876)

Contents

Foreword

There is an overriding need for a new translation of Wagner's libretto to *Der Ring des Nibelungen*: the section entitled 'Translating Wagner's Ring' explains why and also specifies the particular aims of this author's version; for further discussion on the vital topic of the German *Idiom* and the individual language assigned by Wagner to each of his characters the reader is directed to the companion volume of this series.

The main section of this volume – and of the three that cover respectively *Das Rheingold*, *Die Walküre* and *Siegfried* – consists of the German text of the *Ring*, which runs side by side with its English translation. Each leitmotif, as it appears, is indicated in the margin, which also carries the author's annotations on points of particular musical or textual interest. At the beginning of each act is a synopsis of the plot, and a step-by-step breakdown of the action. The leitmotifs new to the act are identified with musical quotations, and there is a brief discussion of the motifs' musical and dramatic character.

In addition to the new translation of Wagner's libretto for the last of the tetralogy, *Götterdämmerung*, this volume provides a brief appreciation of the Wagnerian leitmotif, an introduction to the opera's characters, a presentation of Siegfried's Funeral Music through its leitmotifs and details of who survived and who perished in the cosmic catastrophe that ends the cycle. Appendices include information on the opera's composition and performance, a selective bibliography, discography and videography, and the volume concludes with a comprehensive list of all the leitmotifs that are heard in *Götterdämmerung*.

A number of people have helped me in a number of ways. Hilde Pearton, Dr Maurice Pearton and Stewart Spencer have provided comments in detail and depth. Their generous assistance far exceeds the accepted norm of collegial co-operation, and I hope the present volumes reflect their good counsel. Eric Adler has supplied valuable information about Ring performances in distant climes. The unquenchable thirst for Wagnerian enquiry and intelligence displayed by the students of my seminars on Wagner at Crayford Manor and Higham Hall has been largely responsible for the growth and scope of these five volumes. Several enlightening conversations with Wolfgang Wagner, wise guardian of the Bayreuther Festspiele, have claimed the author's attention and have contributed to smoothing his path through the complexities of the *Ring*.

Emmi Sabor has double-checked the manuscript, and I am grateful for her labour and for the serenity with which she has tolerated Richard Wagner as lodger for the best part of our lives. Lady Young, with Wagnerian seductiveness, was instrumental in persuading Phaidon Press to publish a series of books whose structural and typographical intricacies were formidable. To my editors, Edmund Forey and Ingalo Thomson, and to Hans Dieter Reichert of hdr design, I owe particular thanks for their masterminding of our joint Wagnerian safari.

Rudolph Sabor, Petts Wood, 1997

Leitmotifs: an Introduction

Appreciating the power of Wagner's system of leitmotifs adds a new dimension to our understanding of the *Ring* cycle. There are those who maintain that a leitmotif is little more than a musical visiting card which announces a character's appearance or a dramatic event. This is a fallacy. The Wagnerian leitmotif is an integral element of the *Gesamtkunstwerk*, the totality of the arts – the union of music, poetry and stage craft. It comments on the action, it recalls, it predicts, it even contradicts, occasionally, a character's words or action, but it is always *bona fide*. Leitmotifs are our accredited guides through the profundities of the *Ring*.

To alert the listener to the first appearance of a new leitmotif, Wagner generally repeats it, sometimes more than once, and he frequently prescribes an appropriate action to accompany the motif. A leitmotif undergoes many modifications in the course of the music dramas. It may be varied melodically, rhythmically or harmonically, it may be played by instruments other than those which sounded it at its first appearance. Such modifications are generally inaugurated by either musical or psychological requirements.

Wieland Wagner (1917–66), the composer's grandson, pointed out to his artists that leitmotifs were symbols, and that tracing the course of such musical symbols through the entire *Ring* would amount to a journey of discovery into the realms of depth psychology. Such a course is traced in the companion volume of this series, in the essay 'The Wagnerian Leitmotif'.

The present volumes are committed to defining and interpreting the whole set of motifs, both separately and in the context of the drama, with the aim of equipping the reader with a genuine grasp of the complexities of the work.

Translating Wagner's *Ring*

> Mimi hight a manikin grim,
> who in nought but greed granted me care,
> to count on me, when manful I'd waxed,
> in the wood to slay a worm,
> which long had hidden there a hoard.

More than a hundred years ago the English-speaking world was treated to a translation of the *Ring* by Frederick and Henrietta Corder, husband and wife; the above is a sample of their craft. The Corders had many successors. The most noteworthy are Frederick Jameson in 1896, Margaret Armour in 1911, Ernest Newman in 1912, Stewart Robb in 1960, William Mann in 1964, Peggie Cochrane in 1965, Lionel Salter in 1966, Andrew Porter in 1976 and Stewart Spencer in 1993.

Their translations have much to offer. I have admired and envied many of their neat solutions to intricate problems, and I am indebted to them all for suggesting a phrase here, a telling word there, and for the comfortable assurance of being a successor rather than a pioneer.

So why attempt a new translation? Because Wagner's *Ring*, in spite of minor flaws, is a literary masterpiece, something that none of the existing translations quite manages to convey. But the *Ring* is not only a literary work of art. Its intricate system of metrical patterns, its use of alliteration, its rare but telling rhymes, its imaginative metaphors, its occasional punning, its astonishing ambiguities, its sheer singability – all these combine to create something unique in the history of the opera libretto: the music is in the text. The present translation aims to provide the reader and singer with a libretto which does not sound like a translation, but rather like the text Wagner might have written had he been born not in Leipzig but in London. My objectives are:

– Accuracy
– Matching German and English lines, retaining the position of key words
– Preserving the original metre
– Retaining alliteration and rhyme where possible
– Elucidating where Wagner is obscure
– Emulating the original by allowing each character to speak in his/her particular idiom

Accuracy
Confusion can arise not only from grammatical errors in translation, but also from misunderstood figures of speech; mistranslation can obscure an already complex plot.

Matching Lines and Key Words
To assist the reader, it is essential that the German text and English translation run in parallel; lines must not be transposed just to satisfy grammatical demands. Equally important is the location of key words. Where the German speaks for example of 'Schwert' (sword) or 'Liebe' (love), the word may have been given a particular melodic or instrumental setting, which would be lost if the word were displaced in translation.

Metre
It has earlier been asserted that Wagner's music is already discernible in the text. This is achieved, partly, by the astonishing variety of metre: iambs (.–), trochees (–.), anapests (..–) and spondees (––), long lines and short lines. All coexist without ever disturbing the natural flow of the text.

Alliteration and Rhyme
Wagner regarded alliteration as the textual equivalent of the musical leitmotif. In three of his prose works, *Das Kunstwerk der Zukunft*, *Eine Mitteilung an meine Freunde* and *Oper und Drama*, he stresses the importance of that method of versification which is 'another kind of rhyme'. Indeed, the German term *Stabreim* means 'spelling rhyme'. The counterpart of the *Stabreim* is the true rhyme, which Wagner uses most sparingly in the *Ring*; when he does, it heralds a matter of special importance.

Obscurity and Ambiguity
On the few occasions when Wagner's language is convoluted and the meaning becomes opaque, the translator must lend a helping hand. Wagner's libretto can also include deliberate ambiguity, which must be preserved in the translation.

Characterization
The most important aspect of Wagner's versification is the individual idiom of his characters. Wagner's characterization does not begin on the stage: it is already planned in the language of the text, where each character is given his or her own distinctive mode of expression. It is up to the translator to retrace Wagner's design.

'Poetry is what gets lost in translation,' someone once said. It is the author's sincere wish that this may not be so.

The Story So Far

Das Rheingold

In *Rheingold* Alberich, lord of the subterranean Nibelungs, for-swears love. This enables him to steal the Rhinegold from its careless guardians, the Rhinemaidens. From the gold Alberich forges a ring which makes him, so he thinks, master of the world. The giants Fafner and his brother Fasolt have built a fortress, 'Walhall', for Wotan and his fellow gods. Wotan has promised them as reward Freia, goddess of youth (relying on the cunning of Loge, god of fire, to save her); the giants, hearing about the magic ring fashioned from the gold, wish instead to be rewarded with the gold. They take Freia hostage until Wotan pays the new price. Loge accompanies Wotan to Nibelheim, Alberich's domain, where Mime (Alberich's brother) has fashioned a magic helmet, the Tarnhelm; Alberich is captured by Wotan and Loge and has to buy his freedom with his gold, the Tarnhelm and the ring. Alberich puts a curse on the ring and all its future owners.Wotan offers the gold to the giants as ransom for Freia. But they also demand the Tarnhelm and the ring. Wotan refuses to give them the ring, but Erda, the earth goddess, warns Wotan to yield, adding that the end of the gods is approaching. Wotan obeys, and Fafner kills Fasolt over possession of the ring (the curse is at work!). The gods, led by Wotan, hail the illusory dawn of their power and security, and climb a rainbow bridge which leads to Walhall. Loge foresees the gods' demise and decides not to follow them.

Events between *Das Rheingold* and *Die Walküre*

1. Fafner has turned himself into a dragon, sleeping upon his golden hoard.

2. Travelling to the depths, Wotan has fathered Brünnhilde, his warrior maiden, with Erda.

3. Wotan has fathered another eight daughters, the Valkyries (Walküren), with an unnamed woman, possibly Erda.

4. On a journey to earth, Wotan, with a mortal woman, has fathered the twins Siegmund and Sieglinde.

Die Walküre

Siegmund, pursued by enemies, seeks refuge in Hunding's forest hut. Sieglinde, Hunding's wife, revives the fugitive. They are mutually attracted. Hunding recognizes in Siegmund a deadly enemy. He offers him shelter for the night, but threatens to kill him the next day. When Hunding retires to sleep, Sieglinde shows Siegmund the sword in the tree trunk which had been lodged there by an old man (Wotan). Siegmund withdraws the sword and, realizing who they are, the twin lovers escape. Wotan orders his daughter, Brünnhilde, to aid Siegmund in his battle with Hunding, but Fricka, guardian of wedlock, demands Siegmund's death. Brünnhilde disobeys and causes Wotan to be instrumental in the slaying of Siegmund. Brünnhilde rides away with Sieglinde. She tells her she will give birth to Siegfried, greatest of heroes, and hands her the splinters of Siegmund's sword. Wotan punishes his disobedient daughter by locking her, defenceless, in slumber on a rocky mountain. Yielding to her pleas, Wotan surrounds the rock with a circle of flames which only a fearless hero may penetrate.

Events between *Die Walküre* and *Siegfried*

1. Sieglinde has died giving birth to Siegfried. The splinters of Siegmund's sword have come into Mime's possession.

2. Since Siegfried's birth some eighteen years must be assumed to have elapsed.

3. Mime has brought up Sieglinde's child, expecting him to obtain for him Fafner's hoard and the golden ring.

Siegfried

Mime is unable to forge a sword strong enough for Siegfried to kill Fafner. Wotan, disguised as the Wanderer, tells Mime that Siegmund's shattered sword must be reforged, and that only one who knows no fear can accomplish the task. He adds that Mime's head will be forfeit to such a fearless hero. Being unable to teach Siegfried fear, Mime prepares a poisoned drink, while Siegfried succeeds in reforging his father's sword. Mime leads Siegfried to Fafner's lair and the young hero kills the dragon. Tasting the dragon's blood, Siegfried is able to understand the language of birds. The Woodbird tells him about the treasure and about Mime's duplicity. Siegfried appropriates the Tarnhelm and the ring, and kills Mime. The Woodbird shows him the way to Brünnhilde's rock. Siegfried is confronted by an old man (Wotan) who bars his path. Siegfried shatters his opponent's spear and penetrates the circle of flames. He kisses Brünnhilde awake and makes her his own.

Characters of *Götterdämmerung*

THE THREE NORNS
Weavers of the rope of destiny, seated by the Well of Wisdom underneath the World Ash Tree. They have knowledge of past, present and future. Alto (First Norn), mezzo-soprano (Second Norn) and soprano (Third Norn), in *Götterdämmerung*.

SIEGFRIED
Son of Siegmund and Sieglinde, devised by Wotan as a fearless hero who is to restore the god's fortune. Has killed the dragon and obtained ring and Tarnhelm, has killed Mime, and becomes Brünnhilde's husband. Falls victim to Hagen's intrigues which result in his temporary loss of memory, in his wooing of Gutrune and in his alliance with King Gunther. Disguised by the Tarnhelm, he conquers Brünnhilde on Gunther's behalf, disregards the Rhinemaidens' warning, regains his memory of Brünnhilde and is killed by Hagen. Tenor, in *Siegfried* and *Götterdämmerung*.

BRÜNNHILDE
Valkyrie, daughter of Wotan and Erda. Was punished by Wotan for aiding Siegmund in his battle with Hunding. Is now Siegfried's bride. Receives the cursed ring from him as love token. Is later forced by Siegfried (who has forgotten her) to become King Gunther's bride. Joins in the conspiracy to kill Siegfried. Learns, too late, the truth about Siegfried's Hagen-induced amnesia, returns the ring to the Rhinemaidens and joins the dead Siegfried in the final conflagration. Soprano, in *Walküre*, *Siegfried* and *Götterdämmerung*.

GUNTHER
King of the Gibichungs, brother of Gutrune and half-brother of Hagen, who tricks him into a sham alliance with Siegfried. Receives Brünnhilde from Siegfried's hands, but joins in the plot to kill the hero. Fights with Hagen over possession of the ring and is killed by his deceitful half-brother. Baritone, in *Götterdämmerung*.

GUTRUNE
Sister of Gunther, half-sister of Hagen. Allows herself to be tricked into alliance with Siegfried. Soprano, in *Götterdämmerung*.

HAGEN
Son of Alberich and Queen Grimhild (mother of Gunther and Gutrune). Relentlessly pursues the ring and the Nibelung hoard. Devises Siegfried's temporary amnesia with a magic potion, the hero's alliance with Gutrune, the deception of Brünnhilde and her sham marriage to Gunther. Kills first Siegfried, then Gunther and is drowned by the Rhinemaidens in his final quest for the ring. Bass, in *Götterdämmerung*.

ALBERICH
Father of Hagen, brother of Mime. Ruler of the Nibelungs. Bribed and cajoled Queen Grimhild to bear him a son, Hagen. Wotan created Siegfried in order to restore a status quo; Hagen was created by Alberich for the same reason. Baritone, in *Rheingold, Siegfried* and *Götterdämmerung*.

WALRAUTE
One of the eight Valkyries. Is unsuccessful in persuading Brünnhilde to return the ring to the Rhinemaidens. Forecasts the end of the gods. Mezzo-soprano, in *Walküre* and *Götterdämmerung*.

THREE RHINEMAIDENS
Former guardians of the Rhinegold. Unsuccessful in persuading Siegfried to return the ring, they foretell his imminent death. At the end of the tetralogy they obtain the ring from Brünnhilde's hand. Hagen, who plunges into the river in pursuit of the ring, is drowned by Woglinde and Wellgunde. Soprano (Woglinde), soprano (Wellgunde) and mezzo-soprano (Flosshilde), in *Rheingold* and *Götterdämmerung*.

VASSALS
Hagen's pliant followers. Hagen ensures that they witness Siegfried's alleged betrayal of King Gunther and so will, if necessary, exonerate their master for executing the traitor. Tenors and basses, in *Götterdämmerung*.

WOMEN
Ladies from King Gunther's court and Gutrune's bridesmaids. They briefly comment on Siegfried's alleged treachery and are present at the final conflagration. Sopranos, in *Götterdämmerung*.

Alberich woos Grimhild (mother of
Hagen); illustration by Arthur
Rackham (1911)

Prologue

Synopsis
Leitmotifs
Libretto

Prologue: Story

Brünnhilde's Rock

The Three Norns, weavers of the rope of destiny, discuss events past, present and to come. Wotan, they relate, gave one of his eyes to drink from the Well of Wisdom by the World Ash Tree. He then tore a branch from the tree which he shaped into a mighty spear, engraving it with runes of wisdom. This made him lord of the world. But the tree began to wither and the well dried up. A young hero, Siegfried, later shattered Wotan's spear with his sword. The god then ordered the World Ash Tree to be felled. The Norns also relate the story of the building of Walhall by the giants, and contrast its former glory with its present state, as the immortals and their heroes await the end of the world. The logs that once were the World Ash Tree are heaped around Walhall, and soon Wotan will command Loge to set them alight. The Norns find it increasingly difficult to weave their rope, since Alberich's curse adheres to its strands. As the rope breaks they descend to Erda, their mother.

Day breaks, and Siegfried and Brünnhilde emerge from their cave. She bids him go forth into the world, to fresh adventures. They swear eternal love and fidelity and exchange tokens of love. Siegfried gives Brünnhilde his ring, and she hands over her horse, Grane, to him. Leaving Brünnhilde in the protection of the wall of flames, Siegfried departs. Brünnhilde watches his descent to the Rhine. The orchestral interlude describes his Rhine Journey.

The Norns; illustration by
Arthur Rackham (1911)

Prologue: Action

1. Orchestra: Prelude
2. The Norns
3. Orchestra: Dawn
4. Brünnhilde sends Siegfried into the world
5. Orchestra: Siegfried's Rhine Journey

The Norns as depicted in
Wieland Wagner's 1955
production at Bayreuth

Prologue: Leitmotifs

The leitmotifs new to the Prologue follow in chronological order,
together with the page number of first appearance.

Hero   p.30

Brünnhilde   p.30

Consorts   p.30

Commentary on the Leitmotifs

Hero

With the help of make-up and experience, an actor can easily
age from act to act. Wagner's motifs, with rhythmic modifica-
tion, can do the same. As Siegfried's Horn Call motif (*Siegfried*,
Act I, see below), the motif represented Siegfried's youthful
exuberance:

In its broader rhythm it now characterizes the manly hero.

Brünnhilde

Brünnhilde, too, matures from one drama to the next. In *Walküre* her motif was that of Wotan's Child:

Two dramas later, enriched by the experience of Siegfried's love and possibly foreseeing the tragedy this love will engender, her motif is sombre and pensive. Both motifs are linked by the interval of a seventh: in the motif of Wotan's child it rises, in Brünnhilde's motif it falls.

Consorts

This motif is first heard on the oboe as Brünnhilde shares her brief and final period of unalloyed happiness with Siegfried (in the latter half of the Prologue). Starting on a note foreign to the key and irregular in phrasing and rhythm, its effect is one of intensity, involvement and impetuosity.

Orchestral Prelude

The orchestral opening to *Götterdämmerung*, the prelude to the Prologue, serves as a sombre echo of Brünnhilde's awakening in the third act of *Siegfried*. There, the Revival motif appeared in the bright keys of E minor and C major. Now it is intoned in the gloomy E flat minor and C flat major. In *Siegfried*, Revival spelt hope, but now it suggests a false dawn; then day, now night; then trumpets, now tubas.

The Norns, guardians of fate, no longer weave their rope by the World Ash Tree. That region has suffered environmental ruination ever since Wotan plundered the tree for his spear of power. The Norns now dwell outside Brünnhilde and Siegfried's rocky cave, for these two will now be responsible for the world's fate.

As if to confirm this, with the last of the prelude's Revival chords, tubas sound the Fate motif: 'What is to become of the world?' The orchestral introduction ends with the Death motif on the clarinet; its last bar overlaps with the First Norn's question, 'Welch Licht leuchtet dort?' ('What glow glimmers there?').

Vorspiel

Death

ERSTE NORN
Welch Licht leuchtet dort?

ZWEITE NORN
Loge   Dämmert der Tag schon *auf?*

DRITTE NORN
Loges Heer
Loge   lodert feurig um den Fels.
Noch ist's Nacht.
Was spinnen und singen wir nicht?

ZWEITE NORN
Wollen wir spinnen und
   singen,
woran spannst du das Seil?

ERSTE NORN

So gut und schlimm es geh,
Genesis   schling ich das Seil und *sing*e.
An der Weltesche
wob ich einst,
da gross und stark
dem Stamm entgrünte
weihlicher Äste Wald.
Im kühlen Schatten
rauscht' ein Quell:
Weisheit raunend
rann sein Gewell –
da sang ich heilgen Sinn.
Ein kühner Gott
Walhall   trat zum Trunk an den *Quell*:
seiner Augen eines

Prologue

'I contemplated the Norns' scene with real horror, and for a long time I refused to get involved in it. But now, at last, I have woven this horror into the fabric of the rope, and I admit that it is a unique webbing.' (Wagner to King Ludwig, 5 May 1870)

[Brünnhilde's rock, as at the end of *Siegfried*. Night. Fire glows from below. The Three Norns, weavers of the rope of destiny, are placed by the pine tree (First Norn), by Brünn-hilde's cave (Second) and on the rock (Third).]

FIRST NORN
What glow glimmers there?

SECOND NORN
Dawn of another day!

Rheingold begins with the Rhine-maidens discussing the beginning of the world. *Götterdämmerung* begins with the Norns discussing its ending.

THIRD NORN
Loge's flames
lick and flicker round the fell.
Endless night!
So now let us spin, let us sing.

The Three Fates of Greek Mytho-logy were Lachesis, Klotho and Atropos. Lachesis was responsible for deciding the length of the thread of life, Klotho for spinning it and Atropos for deciding when to cut it.

SECOND NORN
While we are spinning and
    singing,
where will you anchor the rope?

FIRST NORN [rises, unties a golden rope from her body and fastens one end to the pine tree]
For better or for worse,
winding the rope, I sing now.
By the World Ash Tree
once I wove,
when sturdy and strong
the branches burgeoned
into a noble grove.
Its cooling shadows
harboured a spring.
Words of wisdom
welled from the deep,
and sacred was my song.
A dauntless god
came to drink at the spring,
and one eye as forfeit

In Aeschylus' *Prometheus Bound* Wagner encountered this exchange between the Chorus and Prometheus. Chorus: 'Whose hand on the helm controls Neces-sity?' Prometheus: 'The three Fates.' Chorus: 'Has Zeus less power than they?' Prometheus: 'He cannot fly from Fate.'

(Walhall)	zahlt' er als ewigen Zoll.
	Von der Weltesche
Treaty	brach da Wotan einen *Ast*;
	eines Speeres Schaft
	entschnitt' der Starke dem Stamm.
	In langer Zeiten Lauf
	zehrte die Wunde den Wald;
Götterdämmerung	*falb* fielen die Blätter,
	dürr darbte der Baum;
	traurig versiegte
	des Quelles Trank –
	trüben Sinnes
Ring	ward mein Ge*sang*.
	Doch web ich heut
	an der Weltesche nicht mehr,
	muss mir die Tanne
	taugen, zu fesseln das Seil, –
	singe, Schwester,
	dir werf ich's zu:
Death	*weisst* du, wie das wird?

ZWEITE NORN

	Treu beratner
	Verträge Runen
Authority	schnitt *W*otan
	in des Speeres Schaft:
	den hielt er als Haft der Welt.
	Ein kühner Held
	zerhieb im Kampfe den Speer;
	in Trümmer sprang
Walhall	der Verträge heiliger Haft.
	Da hiess Wotan
	Walhalls Helden,
	der Weltesche
Götterdämmerung	*wel*kes Geäst
	mit dem Stamm in Stücke zu
	fällen:
	die Esche sank;
	ewig versiegte der Quell.
	Fessle ich heut
	an dem scharfen Fels das Seil,
	singe, Schwester,
	dir werf ich's zu:
Death	*weisst* du, wie das wird?

DRITTE NORN
Es ragt die Burg,
von Riesen gebaut:

bartered the god for all time.
From the World Ash Ttree
Wotan tore a mighty branch,
and a spear he shaped,
a lordly spear from the stem.
As time and tide grew old,
sickness tormented the grove.
Dry, leafless and ruined,
worn, withered the tree.
Sadly the source
of the spring dried up:
sad my heart
and sadness my song.
Today I weave
by the World Ash Tree no more;
here must the pine tree
serve me to fasten the rope.
Sing, my sister,
take up the cord –
tell us what befalls.

SECOND NORN [winding the rope round
a rock at the entrance to Brünnhilde's cave]
Sacred runes
of trusted treaties
carved Wotan
on the mighty shaft.
It made him the lord all.
A valiant hero
shattered the lordly spear,
and shattered are
all the bonds of gods and of men.
Wotan ordered
Walhall's heroes,
the World Ash Tree's
withering boughs
and its stem to shiver in
    splinters.
The ash tree fell:
spring-water whispered no more.
Now I must bind
to the jagged rock our rope.
Sing, my sister,
take up the cord –
tell us what befalls.

THIRD NORN [takes up the rope]
A rampant fort
the giants had raised.

Siegfrieds Tod (the early version
of *Götterdämmerung*) does not
mention the withering of the
World Ash Tree, and firmly places
the blame for the world's ills on
Alberich. But it hints at a happy
outcome as the Norns gather
their unbroken rope with the
words: 'Wind up the rope, guard it
with care! What we have spun,
binds the world.'

In Siegfried the Norns are men-
tioned, but not seen. Erda advises
Wotan:
    'While I slumber,
    Norns keep vigil.'
Brünnhilde seals her surrender to
Siegfried with the fateful words:
    'You Norns must rend now
    your rope of runes.'
In the present scene the Norns
take Brünnhilde at her word.

In their destructive effect on the
equilibrium of nature Wotan and
Alberich are rivals: Alberich dis-
turbed the primeval order by
plundering the Rhinegold, Wotan
caused the World Ash Tree to
wither.

The Norns' rope is made of gold,
of all metals the most unbidda-
ble. In the Edda Wagner read:
'At night the Norns entered the
hall and allotted life and fate to
him. They spun the thread of his
destiny, and fixed the golden
threads to the sky.'

Götterdämmerung   *Authority*

mit der Götter und Helden
heiliger Sippe
sitzt dort *Wo*tan im Saal.
Gehauner Scheite
hohe Schicht
ragt zu Hauf
rings um die Halle:
die Weltesche war dies einst!
Brennt das Holz
heilig brünstig und hell,
sengt die Glut

Treaty

sehrend den glänzenden *Saal,*

Walhall   *Götterdämmerung*

der ewigen *Göt*ter *En*de

Crisis   *Fate*

dämmert ewig da *auf.*
Wisset ihr noch?
So windet von neuem das Seil;
von Norden wieder
werf ich's dir nach.
Spinne, Schwester, und singe!

Loge

ERSTE NORN
Dämmert der Tag?
Oder leuchtet die Lohe?
Getrübt trügt sich mein Blick;
nicht hell eracht ich
das heilig Alte,
da Loge einst
brannte in lichter Glut.

Death   *Treaty*

Weisst du, was aus ihm ward?

ZWEITE NORN
Durch des Speeres Zauber

Loge

zähmte ihn *Wo*tan;
Räte raunt' er dem Gott:
an des Schaftes Runen,
frei sich zu raten,

Treaty

nagte zehrend sein *Zahn;*
da, mit des Speeres
zwingender Spitze

Loge

bannte ihn *Wo*tan,
Brünnhildes Fels zu umbrennen.

Death   *Authority*

Weisst du, was aus ihm wird?

DRITTE NORN
Des zerschlagnen Speeres

Authority

stechende Splitter
taucht einst Wotan
dem Brünstigen tief in die Brust:
zehrender Brand

With his gods and his heroes,
– august assemblage –
there sits Wotan on high.
A wall of logs
lies heaped aloft,
branch by branch,
all around Walhall.
The World Ash Tree was it once.
When it burns –
sacred tree that it was –
then its flames
feed on the hallowed halls.
The end of the gods, the eternals,
dawns in darkness and doom.
Do you know more?
Then wind we the rope once again.
From northward now
I cast it to you.
Spin, my sister, and sing on!

In Nordic tradition Wotan was not the first trespasser upon the environment. Stags attacked the World Ash Tree and fed on its branches, a serpent gnawed at its roots, a goat at its leaves. But as long as the Norns protect the tree it will not wither.

FIRST NORN
Is that the dawn,
or the flicker of fire?
Alarm outwits my eyes.
I see no longer
those sacred ages,
when Loge would
flare into brilliant flames.
Who knows what was his fate?

In *Siegfrieds Tod* the Third Norn proclaims: 'You Schwarzalben [Nibelungen], be free! Be free, Alberich! Rhinegold, rest in the river!'

SECOND NORN
With his magic spear point
Wotan has tamed him.
Loge counselled the god,
for the runes compelled him.
Then, to escape
he gnawed the shaft of the spear;
but by that spear-point's
spell-binding power,
Wotan compelled him
to make for Brünnhilde's mountain.
What will become of him?

THIRD NORN
The demolished weapon's
transfixing splinters
Wotan plunges
in Loge's smouldering breast.
Furious flames

In the course of this scene the onlooker is treated to a comprehensive recapitulation of previous events. The Norns are decidedly audience-friendly.

		zündet da auf;
		den wirft der Gott
	Walhall	in der *Welt*esche
	Oblivion	zu Hauf geschichtete Scheite.

ZWEITE NORN

	Fate	Wollt ihr *wis*sen,
	Fate	wann das *wird?*
	Grief	*Schwin*get, Schwestern, das Seil!

ERSTE NORN

			Die Nacht weicht;
		Oblivion	nichts mehr ge*wahr* ich;
			des Seiles Fäden
			find ich nicht mehr;
	Oblivion	*Ring*	verflochten ist das Ge*flecht.*
			Ein wüstes Gesicht
Liebe-Tragik	*Rhinegold*	*Joy*	*wirrt* mir wütend den *Sinn:*
			das Rheingold
		Ring	raubte Alberich einst:
			weiss du, was aus ihm *ward?*

ZWEITE NORN

		Des Steines Schärfe
		schnitt in das Seil;
		nicht fest spannt mehr
		der Fäden Gespinst;
		verwirrt ist das Geweb:
		aus Not und Neid
	Grief	ragt mir des Niblungen *Ring:*
		ein rächender Fluch
Gold's Dominion	*Sword*	*nagt* an meiner Fäden Geflecht.
		Weisst du, was daraus wird?

DRITTE NORN

	Zu locker das Seil,
Horn Call	mir langt es nicht.
	Soll ich nach Norden
	neigen das Ende,
	straffer sei es gestreckt!

Curse	Es riss!

ZWEITE NORN
Es riss!

flare from the wound.
These Wotan hurls
at the World Ash Tree,
whose logs are piled around
   Walhall.

SECOND NORN
When shall this be?
Tell us, when?
Wind, o sisters, the rope!

FIRST NORN
The night fades;
dim grows my vision.
No more I find
the strands of the rope;
the threads are tangled and torn.
A sinister scene
mocks and maddens my sight.
The Rhinegold,
seized by Alberich once, –
what did become of him?

SECOND NORN [winding the rope round
the rock]
The jagged rock
has cut through the threads.
The rope anchors
no more as it did.
The strands – knotted and warped!
From grudge and greed
rises the Nibelung's ring.
The curse of that ring
gnaws at the strands of my rope!
What will become of it?

THIRD NORN
Too slack is the rope;
it will not reach.
If to the north
the rope shall be cast,
it must be tighter than this!
[she pulls hard – the rope breaks in
the middle]
It breaks!

SECOND NORN
It breaks!

(Curse)		**ERSTE NORN**
	Götterdämmerung	Es riss!
		DIE DREI NORNEN
Curse		Zu End ewiges Wissen!
		Der Welt melden
	Oblivion	Weise nichts *mehr.*
Oblivion		**DRITTE NORN**
		Hinab!
		ZWEITE NORN
	Fate	Zur Mutter!
		ERSTE NORN
	Fate	Hinab!
Hero	*Brünnhilde*	
Hero	*Ride*	
Hero	*Ride*	
	Brünnhilde	
	Brünnhilde	**BRÜNNHILDE**
		Zu neuen Taten,
		teurer Helde,
		wie liebt ich dich,
		liess ich dich nicht?
		Ein einzig Sorgen
		lässt mich säumen,
	Consorts	dass dir zu *we*nig
		mein Wert gewann.
		Was Götter mich wiesen,
		gab ich dir:
		heiliger Runen
		reichen Hort;
		doch meiner Stärke
		magdlichen Stamm
	Hosanna	nahm *mir* der Held,
	Brünnhilde	dem ich nun mich neige.
		Des Wissens bar,
		doch des Wunsches voll:
		an Liebe reich,
		doch ledig der Kraft,
		mögst du die Arme
		nicht verachten,
	Consorts	die dir nur *gön*nen,
		nicht geben mehr kann!

FIRST NORN
It breaks!

THE THREE NORNS
Now ends knowledge eternal.
The world marks
our wisdom no more.

THIRD NORN
Away!

The end of the news is preceded
by the news of the end.

SECOND NORN
To Erda!

FIRST NORN
Away!
[They vanish. Dawn. The red glow
increases. Sunrise. Broad daylight. Siegfried
and Brünnhilde emerge from the cave. He
is in full armour. She leads her horse by
the bridle.]

In a letter to Nietzsche Cosima
called this orchestral interlude
'the overture to *Götterdämmerung*'. Growing from *pianis-
simo* to *fortissimo*, it conveys the
change from dawn, with its sleeping lovers, to sunlit day, as
Siegfried and Brünnhilde emerge
from their cave. They are accompanied by the Hero, Brünnhilde
and Ride motifs.

BRÜNNHILDE
To purchase honour,
dearest hero,
my love for you
summons you forth.
One sorrow only
now afflicts me:
too small my service,
too weak my worth.
What gods once have taught me,
have I taught:
runes of wisdom's
richest store.
My greatest treasure,
maidenly might,
gave I to him
who is now my master.
In wisdom weak,
but how strong in will;
in love so rich,
in power so poor.
This wretched woman,
do not scorn her.
Her all she granted;
no more can she give.

Brünnhilde's purity of motive in
sending Siegfried out 'to purchase
honour' is tantamount to self-
sacrifice.

In the *Volsunga Saga* Brünnhilde
advises Siegfried: 'Let not fair
women beguile you!' and adds:
'Never swear a false oath! Beware
treacherous friends!'

Brünnhilde is no longer the bold
warrior maid, nor is she now
interested in furthering Wotan's
designs. She has grown into a
woman of great strength of purpose and is full of love.

SIEGFRIED

Consorts

Brünnhilde
Mehr gabst du Wunderfrau,
als ich zu wahren weiss.
Nicht zürne, wenn dein Lehren
mich unbelehret liess!
Ein Wissen doch wahr ich wohl –

Brünnhilde
dass mir Brünnhilde *lebt*;
eine Lehre lernt ich leicht –

Brünnhilde
Brünnhildes zu gedenken.

BRÜNNHILDE

Hero
Willst du mir Minne schenken,
gedenke deiner nur,
gedenke deiner Taten:

Loge + Horn Call
gedenk des wilden Feuers,

Siegfried
das furchtlos du durch*schritt*est,
da den Fels es rings umbrann!

SIEGFRIED

Consorts + Ride   *Hero*
*Brünn*hilde zu ge*win*nen!

BRÜNNHILDE
Gedenk der beschildeten

Ride
   Frau,

Fate
die in tiefem *Schlaf* du fandest,

Siegfried
der *den* festen Helm du erbrachst!

Consorts
SIEGFRIED
Brünnhilde zu erwecken!

Brünnhilde
BRÜNNHILDE
Gedenk der Eide,
die uns einen;
gedenk der Treue,

Consorts
die wir tragen;

Brünnhilde
gedenk der *Lie*be,
der wir leben:
Brünnhilde brennt dann ewig

Bequest
heilig dir in der *Brust.*

SIEGFRIED

Hero
Lass ich dich, Liebste, hier
in der Lohe heiliger Hut,
zum Tausche deiner Runen

Ring
reich ich dir diesen *Ring*.

Siegfried
Was *der* Taten je ich schuf,
des Tugend schliesst er ein.

SIEGFRIED
More, you my heart's delight,
you gave than I can grasp.
So chide not, if your teaching
has left me still untaught.
Yet, one lesson have I learnt:
I am Brünnhilde's life.
One command I hold in mind:
Brünnhilde to remember.

BRÜNNHILDE
If you do truly love me,
be mindful of your life.
Your dauntless deeds remember;
recall the raging fire.
No fear defied the hero,
as it flamed around the fell.

SIEGFRIED
Brünnhild, my heart's desire!

BRÜNNHILDE
Remember the shield-sheltered
    maid,
whom you found there, lapped in
    slumber,
and whose fastened helmet you
    loosed.

SIEGFRIED
Brünnhilde to awaken!

BRÜNNHILDE
The oath remember
that unites us.
The pledge remember
that we plighted.
The love remember
that we live for.
Then Brünnhild burns for ever,
hallowed, deep in your heart.

This passage echoes the final
scene of *Siegfried*. The two lovers
relive their ecstatic union at a
feverish pitch, as if knowing that
their love is doomed.

SIEGFRIED
You, beloved, I leave
in the sacred fastness of fire.
For all that you have taught me,
I now give you this ring.
All the tasks I have performed,
reside within this ring;

Two harps signify the couple's
togetherness, illusory though it is,
at this climactic moment.

Another echo of the *Siegfried*
finale is provided by the Bequest
motif which, according to Wagner,
should strike the listener 'like the
proclamation of a new religion'.

Hero + Dragon		Ich er*schlug* einen wilden Wurm,
		der grimmig lang ihn bewacht:
		nun wahre du seine Kraft
	Ring	als Weihegruss meiner Treu!

BRÜNNHILDE

Ride	*Consorts*	*Ihn geiz* ich als einziges Gut!
Rhinegold		Für den Ring nimm nun auch
	Ride	mein *Ross*!
		Ging sein Lauf mit mir
		einst kühn durch die Lüfte,
		mit mir
		verlor es die mächtge Art;
		über Wolken hin
		auf blitzenden Wettern
		nicht mehr
	Ride	schwingt es sich mutig des Wegs;
		doch wohin du ihn führst,
		sei es durchs Feuer,
	Hero	*grau*enlos folgt dir Grane:
		denn dir, o Helde,
		soll er gehorchen.
		Du hüt ihn wohl; er hört dein
	Liebesnot	Wort:
		O, bringe Grane
Consorts	*Ride*	*oft* Brünnhildes *Gruss*!

SIEGFRIED

		Durch deine Tugend allein
	Ride	soll so ich Taten noch *wirken*?
		Meine Kämpfe kiesest du,
		meine Siege kehren zu dir:
		auf deines Rosses Rücken,
		in deines Schildes Schirm,
	Freedom	*nicht* Siegfried acht ich mich mehr,
Ride	*Consorts*	ich bin nur *Brünn*hildes *Arm*.

BRÜNNHILDE

	Freedom	O wäre Brünnhild deine *See*le!

SIEGFRIED

	Consorts	Durch sie entbrennt mir der *Mut*.

BRÜNNHILDE

		So wärst du Siegfried und
	Consorts	Brünnhild?

I have fought a dragon fiend,
who paid with his life for the ring.
Now make its virtue your strength:
a sacred vow of my troth.

BRÜNNHILDE
I covet it more than my life!
For the ring take my sterling
    steed!
Though he used to fly
with me through the storm clouds,
with me
he lost all his magic might.
Through the clouds, through sky,
through thunder and lightning
no more
lordly aloft will he soar.
But the course you command,
be it through fire,
fearlessly Grane will follow.
Beloved hero,
he shall obey you.
Take care of him; he cares for
    you;
and often give him
fond greetings from me.

SIEGFRIED
It is your virtue alone
sustains me now in my ventures.
All my battles you shall bless;
all my honours are but your own.
When on your steed I am mounted,
when sheltered by your shield,
then Siegfried am I no more:
I am but Brünnhilde's arm.

BRÜNNHILDE
O were but Brünnhild your own
    spirit!

SIEGFRIED
She kindles my courage anew!

BRÜNNHILDE
Then you are Siegfried and
    Brünnhild?

The simultaneous sounding of the Hero and Dragon motifs is deceptively unambiguous. Wagner points to Siegfried's slaying of the dragon, but also alludes to a link between the Dragon and Brünnhilde. The curse-laden ring has reawoken the dragon in her.

This pledge of love is heavy with Alberich's curse. It will not save Brünnhilde from dishonour nor Siegfried from death.

Grane for the ring is a fatal exchange, as the ring proves ineffectual. The horse might have offered Brünnhilde better protection.

Moritz Wirth, a German musicologist of the late nineteenth century, discovered that Brünnhilde was pregnant when Siegfried left her. With the help of a gynaecologist he even detected the hitherto unsuspected 'First-thrust-of-the-infant-in-the-womb motif'.

In their reciprocal self-identification and self-surrender, Siegfried and Brünnhilde discuss a philosophical proposition which had already been searchingly examined in *Tristan und Isolde*.

SIEGFRIED

Freedom Wo ich bin, bergen sich *Bei*de.

BRÜNNHILDE

So verödet mein Felsensaal?

SIEGFRIED

Hero Vereint fasst er uns *Zwei*!

BRÜNNHILDE

Freedom *Brünnhilde* *O*! heilige *Göt*ter!
Hehre Geschlechter!
Weidet eu'r Aug
an dem weihvollen Paar!
Freedom *Brünnhilde* *Freedom* Ge*trennt* – wer will es scheiden?
Consorts Geschieden – trennt es sich nie!

SIEGFRIED

Freedom *Heil* dir, Brünnhilde,
prangender Stern!
Heil, strahlende Liebe!

BRÜNNHILDE

Heil dir, Siegfried,
Brünnhilde *Freedom* *sie*gendes Licht!
Heil, strahlendes Leben!

BEIDE

Ride *Heil*! Heil! Heil! Heil!

Hero *Freedom* *Brünnhilde* *Hosanna* *Brünnhilde* *Hosanna*
Horn Call *Brünnhilde* *Horn Call* *Liebesnot* *Liebesbund*
Horn Call *Loge* *Liebesbund* *Genesis* *Götterdämmerung*
Genesis *Joy + Horn Call* *Joy* *Liebe-Tragik* *Ring*
Rhinegold *Grief* *Gold's Dominion*

SIEGFRIED
Where I am, both are united.

BRÜNNHILDE
Then forlorn shall be Brünnhild's
fell?

SIEGFRIED
My heart leave I behind!

BRÜNNHILDE
O heavenly gods,
o hallowed eternals!
Smile at the sight
of our sanctified love!
Apart – who shall divide us?
Divided – never to part!

SIEGFRIED
Hail, my Brünnhilde,
radiant star!
Hail, love in its glory!

BRÜNNHILDE
Hail, my Siegfried,
conquering light!
Hail, life in its glory!

BOTH
Hail! Hail! Hail! Hail!
[Siegfried leads Grane quickly towards the
edge of the rock. Brünnhilde follows him and
watches his descent. She hears Siegfried's
horn call and greets him with ecstatic
gestures. The curtain falls swiftly.]

Siegfried's protestations of love
and fidelity have an ominous ring:
'More … you gave than I can
grasp.'; 'Siegfried am I no more.';
'My heart leave I behind.'
Even more alarming are the recur-
rent warnings expressed by the
Freedom motif – freedom to
wander and freedom from
togetherness.

In his theoretical writings Wagner
rejected the 'old-fashioned' duet.
Yet here, the practical musician in
him gives us a duet in all but
name. Moreover, he lets
Brünnhilde finish with a glorious,
albeit very 'old-fashioned' high C.

When Siegfried leaves
Brünnhilde's (and the Norns')
rock for the Gibichung court he
steps from the superterrestial
realm to the haunts of men, from
myth to history.

Wagner gives very precise stage
directions for Siegfried's departure on his Rhine Journey. In fact,
the motifs themselves tell the
story in almost equal detail:
'Siegfried leads Grane towards
the edge of the rock [Hero motif],
followed by Brünnhilde. Hero and
horse descend and are no longer
seen by the audience [Freedom].
Brünnhilde, now alone, gazes
after them [Brünnhilde and
Hosanna]. Siegfried's horn is
heard from the valley below
[Horn Call]. Brünnhilde listens.
She steps closer to the edge and,
seeing Siegfried down below,
waves delightedly [Liebesbund].'

The curtain falls, while the music
continues to describe Siegfried's
journey. He re-crosses the protec-
tive wall of flames [Loge] and
reaches the Rhine [Genesis].
There he finds a boat and, with
Grane as passenger, he rows
upstream, towards the joyless
domain of Gunther, King of the
Gibichungs, and his half-brother,
Hagen, son of Alberich. The
motifs of this final section – Götterdämmerung, Liebe-Tragik, Ring,
Rhinegold, Grief and Gold's
Dominion – gloomily predict the
fate of Siegfried's journey.

Waltraute implores Brünnhilde
to return the ring to the Rhine;
illustration by Franz Stassen
(c. 1910)

I
Act

Synopsis
Leitmotifs
Libretto

Act 1: Story

The Hall of the Gibichungs

Scene 1
The feeble King Gunther, lord of the Gibichungs, asks Hagen, his half-brother, to assist him in his quest for prestigious ventures. Hagen, son of Alberich and Gunther's mother, advises him and his half-sister Gutrune to make advantageous marriages.

Scene 2
Siegfried arrives at Gunther's court. Hagen causes Siegfried to fall in love with Gutrune by means of a potion which makes him forget Brünnhilde. Prompted by Hagen, Siegfried promises Gunther to obtain Brünnhilde for him. They seal their plot with an oath of bloodbrotherhood and immediately set out on their quest. Hagen remains behind, guarding the hall, and confidently awaiting the outcome of the plot – his possession of the ring.

Scene 3
Waltraute, Brünnhilde's sister and former fellow-Valkyrie, has secretly left Walhall to visit Brünnhilde. She implores her to return the ring to the Rhine in order to lift Alberich's curse, which is responsible for the present state of the gods who are passively awaiting their downfall. The logs of the former World Ash Tree, she reports, are heaped around Walhall, ready to be ignited by Loge. Brünnhilde refuses to part with Siegfried's token of love, and she sends her sister away. Siegfried, disguised as Gunther (with the help of the Tarnhelm) penetrates the wall of flames and wrests the ring from Brünnhilde. He forces her into her chamber but, true to his oath, places his sword between himself and Brünnhilde.

Siegfried: 'This drink, my love,
with love undying, Brünnhilde,
shall be yours!' Act I of *Götterdämmerung* in the Berlin
production of 1907

Act I: Action

Siegfried tries to take the ring from Brünnhilde: 'To ravish the ring I learn from your lips.'

Act I: Leitmotifs

The leitmotifs new to the act follow in chronological order, together with the page number of first appearance.

Hagen   p.46

Gibichungen   p.46

Amnesia   p.52

Gutrune   p.60

Bloodbrothers   p.64

Revenge   p.76

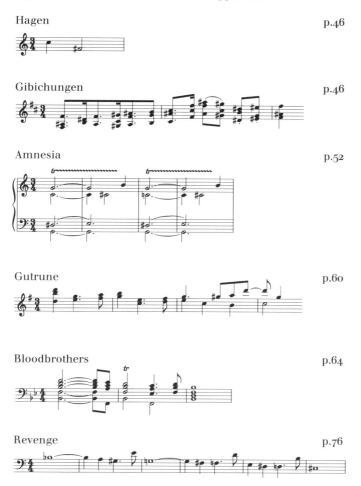

Commentary on the Leitmotifs

Hagen

A falling interval, usually beginning with an accented upper note, characterizes this two-note motif. The interval may be anything between a third and over an octave. Its elusiveness matches its subject. At its most sinister it descends by an augmented fourth, the 'diabolus in musica'.

Gibichungen

The full motif stretches over eight bars, but it is normally heard in this shorter version. The insistent dotted rhythm conveys the obsessions of those lords and ladies of deceit – Gunther's with prestige, Gutrune's with a husband, and Hagen's with the ring.

Amnesia

Although the Amnesia motif is first heard before Siegfried's arrival at Gunther's court, we hear its full version when Gutrune welcomes Siegfried with her drink of oblivion. Shifting horn harmonies are accompanied by violin trills. This is psychologically remarkable: a trill is a note which constantly disowns itself.

Gutrune

Musically, this is an inversion of the Horn Call which was heard at Siegfried's departure from Brünnhilde. Dramatically, it marks Siegfried's *mésalliance* with his greedy new friend's greedy sister.

Bloodbrothers

A strong, diatonic motif of a seeming probity that invites comparison to a Judas kiss. It only occurs a few times in *Götterdämmerung*, but when it does, beware.

Revenge

A doom-laden motif, heavy with chromatic notes and sinister intervals, rising and falling. It sounds during the fateful interview between Brünnhilde and Waltraute; at Brünnhilde's discovery of the ring on Siegfried's finger; at the end of the conspirators' trio (Hagen–Gunther–Brünnhilde); and when Siegfried's body is carried into Gunther's hall.

I. Akt: 1. Szene

<table>
<tr><td>Hagen</td><td>GUNTHER</td></tr>
<tr><td>Gibichungen⌉</td><td>Nun hör, Hagen;</td></tr>
<tr><td></td><td>sage mir, Held:</td></tr>
<tr><td></td><td>sitz ich herrlich am Rhein</td></tr>
<tr><td></td><td>Gunther zu Gibichs Ruhm?</td></tr>
</table>

                                    HAGEN

Hagen — Dich *echt* genannten

Hagen Gibichungen⌉ — *acht* ich zu *nei*den;

die beid uns Brüder gebar,

Ring — Frau Grim*hild liess* mich's
      begreifen.

Gibichungen⌉ — GUNTHER
Dich neide ich;
nicht neide mich du.

Hagen⌉ — Erbt ich Erstlings *Art*,
Weisheit ward dir allein:
Halbbrüder Zwist
bezwang sich nie besser.

Hagen — Deinem *Rat* nur *red* ich Lob

Gibichungen   *Gold's Dominion*   *frag* ich dich nach meinem Ruhm.

HAGEN
Hagen — So schelt ich den Rat,
Freia — da schlecht noch dein *Ruhm*;
denn hohe Güter weiss ich,
die der Gibichung noch nicht
      gewann.

GUNTHER
Verschwiegst du sie,
so schelt auch ich.

Act I: Scene 1

[The Hall of the Gibichungs on the Rhine.
At the back is an open view to the river bank.
Gunther and Gutrune, enthroned. Hagen
sits aside.]

GUNTHER
Now speak, Hagen,
tell me the truth:
does my rule along the Rhine
flatter my father's fame?

HAGEN
Your true-born status
strikes me with envy;
and she who bore you and me,
Frau Grimhild, bade me respect it.

GUNTHER
I envy you,
so envy not me!
Mine the first-born's fame,
wisdom is your bequest.
Halfbrothers' feud
can never afflict us.
Your own shrewdness wins
    my praise,
when I question my prestige.

HAGEN
Then I am to blame:
your laurels are lean.
I know of treasured trophies
unobtained as yet by Gibich's
    son.

GUNTHER
Conceal them not,
or take the blame!

'I question my prestige.' The
shabby dealings used in pursuit
of such a supposedly Germanic
virtue as 'prestige' tend to de-
value its appeal.

HAGEN
In sommerlich reifer Stärke

seh ich Gibichs Stamm,
dich, Gunther, unbeweibt,
dich, Gutrun, ohne Mann.

Hagen   *Freia*

GUNTHER
Wen rätst du nun zu frein,

Gibichungen   *Ride*   dass unsrem Ruhm es *frommt*?

HAGEN
Ein Weib weiss ich,

Loge   das herrlichste der Welt;
auf Felsen hoch ihr Sitz;

Woodbird   ein *Feuer* umbrennt ihren Saal:
nur, wer durch das Feuer
    bricht,
darf Brünnhildes Freier sein.

GUNTHER
Ride   *Gibichungen*   *Hagen*   Vermag *das mein* Mut zu bestehn?

HAGEN
Einem Stärkren noch ist's nur
    bestimmt.

GUNTHER
Wer ist der streitlichste Mann?

HAGEN
Siegfried, der Wälsungen Spross,

Nothung   *Wälsungen*   *der* ist der stärkste *Held*.
Ein Zwillingspaar,
von Liebe bezwungen,
Siegmund und Sieglinde
zeugten den echtesten Sohn.

Horn Call   Der im *Wal*de mächtig
    erwuchs,
den wünsch ich Gutrun zum
    Mann.

GUTRUNE
Welche Tat schuf er so tapfer,
dass als herrlichster Held er
    genannt?

HAGEN
In summer's full prime and
  ripeness
prospers Gibich's race;
but Gunther has no wife;
you, Gutrun, are unwed.

GUNTHER
Whom would you have me wed,
to profit our prestige?

HAGEN
A rare woman,
unrivalled in this world:
on soaring fell her home,
a fire encircles her hall;
but he who can brave the
  flames,
is Brünnhilde's conquering lord.

GUNTHER
And have I the strength for the
  task?

HAGEN
To a stronger man she is ordained.

GUNTHER
Who is this valorous man?

HAGEN
Siegfried, the Wälsungen-son,
he is that mighty man.
A twin-born pair,
by love overmastered,
Siegmund and Sieglind,
engendered just such a son.
In the woods he grew sturdy and
  strong.
This hero Gutrun should wed.

GUTRUNE
In what battles did he prosper,
to be hailed as the mightiest of
  men?

Even before Hagen has mentioned the name of Gunther's prospective bride, the listener knows her identity, thanks to the Ride, Loge and Woodbird motifs.

We read in Cosima's diaries (7 February 1870) that Wagner likened the gloomy Gibichung court to 'a gathering of wild beasts, of lions, tigers etc., who devour each other.'

Wagner instructs Gutrune to 'begin shyly', and her words are preceded by a virginal oboe solo. Events will show that innocence alone is no shield against corruption.

		HAGEN
Dragon		Vor *Neid*höhle
		den Niblungenhort
Ring		be*wachte* ein riesiger Wurm:
Fafner		*Sieg*fried schloss ihm
		den freislichen Schlund,
		erschlug ihn mit siegendem
		Schwert.
		Solch ungeheurer Tat
Sword	*Horn Call*	ent*rag*te des Helden *Ruhm.*

	GUNTHER
Ring	Vom *Nib*lungenhort vernahm
	ich:
	er birgt den neidlichsten Schatz?

	HAGEN
	Wer wohl ihn zu nützen wüsst,
Liebe-Tragik *Rhinegold*	dem *neig*te sich wahr*lich* die Welt.

	GUNTHER
Rhinegold	Und Sieg*fried* – hat ihn erkämpft?

	HAGEN
Grief *Gold's Dominion*	*Knecht* sind die Niblungen *ihm.*

GUNTHER
Und Brünnhild gewänne nur er?

	HAGEN
Ride	*Kei*nem andren wiche die Brunst.

	GUNTHER
	Was weckst du Zweifel und Zwist,
	Was ich nicht zwingen soll,
	darnach zu verlangen
Gibichungen	machst du mir Lust?

Tarnhelm	HAGEN
	Brächte Siegfried
	die Braut dir heim,
Gibichungen	wär dann nicht Brünnhilde *dein*?

GUNTHER
Was zwänge den frohen Mann
für mich die Braut zu frein?

HAGEN
At *Neidhöhle*,
the Nibelung hoard
was guarded by Fafner, the fiend.
Siegfried stopped up
his terrible jaw,
and slew him with conquering
    sword.
Such deed, such daring deed
has won him a hero's name.

GUNTHER
The Nibelung hoard, one
    whispers,
contains most coveted wealth.

HAGEN
The man who controls its charm,
commands the control of the world.

GUNTHER
And Siegfried won it himself?

HAGEN
Lord of the Niblungen he.

GUNTHER
And Brünnhild would yield but to
    him?

HAGEN
He alone can master the flames.

GUNTHER [rises angrily]
Why rouse desire and doubt?
Why will you let me crave
    forbidden fruits
and dreams of delight?

HAGEN
But, should Siegfried
bring home the bride,
would not Brünnhilde be yours?

GUNTHER
What power could charm that man
to woo the bride for me?

'Neidhöhle' means 'cavern of greed'.

Hagen's recapitulation of past events – the story of the Wälsungen, of the dragon, of Brünnhilde and of Siegfried – is not only for the benefit of the Gibichung court but for the audience as well.

In telling Siegfried's story, Hagen simultaneously whets Gunther's appetite for Siegfried's possessions and Gutrune's appetite for Siegfried himself.

HAGEN
Ihn zwänge bald deine Bitte,
bänd ihn Gutrun zuvor.

GUTRUNE
Du Spötter, böser Hagen!
Wie sollt ich Siegfried binden?
Ist er der herrlichste
Held der Welt,
der Erde holdeste Frauen
friedeten längst ihn schon.

HAGEN
Gedenk des Trankes im Schrein;
vertraue mir, der ihn gewann:
den Helden, des du verlangst,

Liebe-Tragik + Freia *bind*et er liebend an dich.
Sword Träte nun Siegfried ein,
Tarnhelm genöss er des würzigen Tranks
Freia dass vor dir ein Weib er er*sah,*
dass je ein Weib ihm genaht,
Amnesia *Hagen* ver*ges*sen müsst er des ganz.
Nun redet:
Gold's Dominion wie *dünkt* euch Hagens Rat?

GUNTHER
Gibichungen Gepriesen sei Grimhild,
Hagen die uns den Bruder gab!

GUTRUNE
Hagen Möcht ich Siegfried je ersehn!

GUNTHER
Curse *Hagen* *Horn Call* Wie fänden ihn wir *auf?*
Treasure

HAGEN
Horn Call *Jagt* er auf Taten
wonnig umher,
zum engen Tann
wird ihm die Welt:
wohl stürmt er in rastloser
Jagd
auch zu Gibichs Strand an den
Rhein.

GUNTHER
Horn Call *Hagen* Willkommen hiess ich ihn gern.

HAGEN
The charm of Gunther's appeal,
the power of Gutrune's charm.

GUTRUNE
You mock me, wicked Hagen!
How could I charm that hero?
Is he the lordliest
lord of all,
then all the winsomest women
lavished on him their love.

HAGEN
The potion – have you forgot?
Have faith in me; I know its charm.
The hero whom you desire,
he shall be bound to your heart.
Hither let Siegfried come
and drink the magical draught:
he forgets all women but you,
forgets all beauty but yours,
forgets – forgets – has forgot.
Now answer:
is Hagen's plan approved?

GUNTHER
All praise be to Grimhild,
for such a son as this!

GUTRUNE
Would but Siegfried pass this way!

GUNTHER
How can we seek him out?
[a horn is heard, loudly but far off]

HAGEN
He hunts for glory
throughout the world.
Too quiet that world
for Siegfried's quest.
That quest will soon make him
    seek out
glorious Gibich's realm on the
    Rhine.

GUNTHER
Welcome, whenever he will.
[both listen to a horn call]

Hagen ensnares Gutrune with a
devilish mixture of motifs: Freia
(cello) and Tarnhelm (horns), saying in effect: 'You can buy
Siegfried's love by fraud.'

The potion's true function is not
causal but illustrative: Siegfried,
alas, is ready for fresh encounters.
Not for nothing had Brünnhilde
sent him out 'zu neuen Taten' (to
fresh adventures).

(Hagen) Vom Rhein her tönt das Horn!

Grief

Hagen

Horn Call *Joy*

HAGEN
In einem Nachen Held und Ross!
Der bläst so munter das *Horn*!
Ein gemächlicher Schlag,
wie von müssiger Hand,
treibt jach den Kahn
wider den Strom:
so rüstiger Kraft
Sword in des Ruders Schwung
rühmt sich nur der,
der den Wurm erschlug.
Ring Siegfried ist es, sicher kein Andrer!

GUNTHER
Jagt er vorbei?

HAGEN
Hoiho! Wohin,
du heitrer Held?

SIEGFRIEDS STIMME
Gibichungen Zu Gibichs starkem *Soh*ne.

HAGEN
Gibichungen Zu seiner Halle entbiet ich dich.

Hierher! Hier lege an!

A horn rings out from the Rhine!
[Hagen has gone to the river bank and
calls back to Gunther]

HAGEN
I see a vessel! Man and horse!
He blows that boisterous horn!
Such an effortless stroke,
and such leisurely hands
hurl on the boat,
braving the waves.
So skilful an arm,
as he plies his oars.
This is the arm   .
that had felled the foe.
Siegfried is it, he and no other!

GUNTHER
Will he speed by?

HAGEN
Hoiho! Where to,
my hero, speak?

SIEGFRIED [from the river]
I seek the son of Gibich.

HAGEN
His hall awaits you. Be welcome
    here.
[Siegfried appears in his boat by the bank]
This way! Here come ashore!

Siegfried's jaunty Horn Call is
answered by the sullen falling
fifth of the Hagen motif of cellos
and horn.

Hagen prepares to welcome
Siegfried with his fatal potion. The
three cello notes, F, G flat and C,
are the same notes that are heard
in *Tristan und Isolde*, when the
lovers' fatal potion is brewed and
offered.

I. Akt: 2. Szene

HAGEN

Curse   *Crisis*   *Siegfried*   *Heil! Heil* Siegfried, teurer Held!

SIEGFRIED
Wer ist Gibichs Sohn?

GUNTHER

Gibichungen   Gunther, ich, den du suchst.

SIEGFRIED

Siegfried   Dich hört *ich* rühmen
weit am Rhein:
Horn Call   *nun* ficht mit mir,
oder sei mein Freund!

GUNTHER
Lass den Kampf!
Crisis   Sei willkommen!

Ride   SIEGFRIED
Wo berg ich mein Ross?

HAGEN
Curse   Ich biet ihm Rast.

SIEGFRIED
Curse   Du riefst mich Siegfried:
sahst du mich schon?

HAGEN
Ich kannte dich nur
Ride   an deiner Kraft.

Act I: Scene 2

[Hagen fastens the boat. Siegfried leaps
ashore, leading his horse.]

HAGEN
Hail! Siegfried, hero, hail!
[Gunther joins Hagen on the river bank.
Gutrune watches Siegfried in wonder and
admiration.]

SIEGFRIED
Who is Gibich's son?

GUNTHER
Gunther, I whom you seek.

SIEGFRIED
Your name is famed
along the Rhine.
Now fight with me,
or else be my friend!

GUNTHER
Speak of peace
and be welcome!

SIEGFRIED
Who'll stable my horse?

HAGEN
Leave him to me.

SIEGFRIED
You called me *Siegfried*?
Strangers are we!

HAGEN
I witnessed your strength
and knew your name.

Hagen welcomes Siegfried with
sham respect. The orchestra, as
always, tells the truth: three trombones issue a warning with their
Curse motif.

At his entry Siegfried is
represented by four horns playing
his motif *forte*; low trumpets and
trombones, *piano*, seem almost
ashamed to sound the weak Gunther's weak Gibichungen motif.

In the *Nibelungenlied* Siegfried
wisely intends not to stay long
enough at Gunther's court for his
horse to need stabling.

		SIEGFRIED
	Brünnhilde⌐	Wohl hüte mir *Grane*:
		du hieltest nie
Consorts	Ride⌐	von edlerer *Zucht*
	Crisis	am Zaume ein Ross.

		GUNTHER
	Hagen	Begrüsse froh, o Held,
		die Halle meines Vaters:
		wohin du schreitest,
		was du ersiehst,
		das achte nun dein Eigen;
		dein ist mein Erbe,
		Land und Leut:
		hilf, mein Leib, meinem Eide!
	Hagen	*Mich* selbst geb ich zum Mann.

		SIEGFRIED
		Nicht Land noch Leute biete ich,
Wälsungen	Jubilation	noch Vaters Haus und Hof:
		einzig erbt ich
		den eignen Leib –
	Action	lebend zehr ich den *auf.*
Sword	Forge	Nur ein Schwert hab *ich*,
		selbst geschmiedet:
	Hagen	*hilf*, mein Schwert, meinem *Ei*de!
Hagen + Treasure	Forge	Das biet ich mit mir zum *Bund.*

HAGEN
Doch des Niblungenhortes
nennt die Märe dich Herrn?

SIEGFRIED
Des Schatzes vergass ich fast;
so schätz ich sein müssges Gut!

Dragon⌐	In einer *Höhl*e liess ich's liegen,
	wo ein Wurm es einst bewacht.

HAGEN
Und nichts entnahmst du ihm?

SIEGFRIED

Dies Gewirk, unkund seiner Kraft.

SIEGFRIED
Take good care of Grane!
You never yet
have led by the rein
so noble a horse.
[Hagen leads the horse away. Gutrune
leaves, at Hagen's silent command. Siegfried does not notice this. Gunther beckons
to Siegfried, and they step forward into
the hall.]

GUNTHER
I greet my welcome guest
within the hall of my father.
The ground you stand on,
all that you see,
treat now as your own chattel.
Yours is my kingdom,
fields and folk:
let my life be my warrant!
Myself you shall command.

SIEGFRIED
Nor fields nor folk have I to grant,
nor father's house and hall.
All my wealth is
my life and limbs:
these I waste as I live.
See this sword, Gunther,
I have forged it:
let my sword be my warrant!
This and myself shall be yours.

HAGEN [has returned]
But the Nibelung's ransom –
rumour names you its lord?

SIEGFRIED
I almost forgot the gold.
It means very little to me.
In a lair I left it lying,
where a dragon once kept watch.

HAGEN
And you took none of it?

SIEGFRIED [pointing to the cap of mail that
hangs from his belt]
Just this thing, which I cannot use.

In the prose sketch to *Siegfrieds Tod* Gunther stoops lower still: 'You be master here, and all of us shall be your slaves.'

As Hagen stables Grane, grumbling bassoons, horns and double basses portray the noble beast's annoyance with its sinister groom.

Siegfried knows nothing of the Tarnhelm's magic power. This reminds us of Mime, who declares in *Rheingold*: 'I only forged the helm, but – the magic that lurks inside, that magic I cannot unlock.'

HAGEN
Den Tarnhelm kenn ich,
der Niblungen künstliches Werk:
er taugt, bedeckt er dein Haupt,
dir zu tauschen jede Gestalt;
verlangt dich's an fernsten Ort,
er entführt flugs dich dahin.
Sonst nichts entnahmst du dem
Hort?

Tarnhelm

Forge

Ring

SIEGFRIED
Einen Ring.

Consorts

HAGEN
Den hütest du wohl?

SIEGFRIED
Den hütet ein hehres Weib.

HAGEN
*Brünn*hild!

Hagen

GUNTHER
Nicht, Siegfried, sollst du mir
*tau*schen.
Tand gäb ich für dein Geschmeid,
nähmst all mein Gut du dafür:
ohn Entgelt dien ich dir gern.

Hagen

Gutrune

GUTRUNE
Willkommen, Gast,
in Gibichs Haus!
Seine Tochter reicht dir den Trank.

Gutrune

SIEGFRIED
*Ver*gäss ich Alles,
was du mir gabst,
von einer Lehre
lass ich doch nie:
den ersten Trunk
zu treuer Minne,
Brünnhilde, bring ich dir!

Hosanna

Bequest

Amnesia *Gutrune*

HAGEN
The Tarnhelm is it,
the Nibelungs' cunning device!
It serves, when set on your head,
to transform you at your command;
or if you would be elsewhere,
you can fly whither you will.
No more you took from the hoard?

The Tarnhelm confers three powers: instantaneous transportation, changing of shape and invisibility. Its predecessors in this last power were Gyges' ring, Boccaccio's Heliotrope, Perseus' helmet and Reynard's ring.

SIEGFRIED
Just one ring.

HAGEN
You guard it with care?

SIEGFRIED
A woman guards it with care.

HAGEN [aside]
Brünnhild!

GUNTHER
No, Siegfried, let us not
    barter.
Trash, trifles and toys were yours,
if you accept all I own.
I'll gladly serve you as friend.
[Hagen opens Gutrune's door. She now
enters, bearing a drinking-horn with which
she approaches Siegfried.]

GUTRUNE
Be welcome, guest,
in Gibich's house.
Let his daughter bring you this
    drink.

Harp sounds bewitched Siegfried's ears and heart at Brünnhilde's awakening in the third act of *Siegfried*. They bewitch him again now, as Gutrune enters.

SIEGFRIED [bows to her politely]
Were all forgot
you granted to me,
one sacred lesson
lives in my heart:
this drink, my love,
with love undying,
Brünnhilde, shall be yours!
[He drinks, then returns the horn to Gutrune
who lowers her eyes before him in shame
and confusion. He now looks at her with
suddenly inflamed passion.]

Muted horns deaden Siegfried's memory.

(Gutrune) Die so mit dem Blitz
den Blick du mir sengst,
was senkst du dein Auge vor mir?
Ha, schönstes Weib!
Schliesse den Blick;
das Herz in der Brust
brennt mir sein Strahl,
zu feurigen Strömen fühl ich
ihn zehrend zünden mein Blut!

Gutrune Gunther, wie heisst deine Schwester?

GUNTHER
Gutrune Gutrune.

SIEGFRIED
Gutrune Sind's gute Runen,
die ihrem Aug ich entrate?

Deinem Bruder bot ich mich zum
   Mann:
der Stolze schlug mich aus;
trügst du wie er mir Übermut,
Hagen   *Gutrune*   *Curse* böt ich mich dir zum Bund?

SIEGFRIED
Hagen Hast du, Gunther, ein *Weib*?

GUNTHER
Nicht freit ich noch,
und einer Frau
Ride soll ich mich schwerlich freun:
Gold's Dominion auf Eine setzt ich den *Sinn*,
Hagen die kein *Rat* mir je gewinnt.

SIEGFRIED
Jubilation Was wär dir versagt,
Loge steh ich zu dir?

GUNTHER
Loge Auf Felsen hoch ihr Sitz

SIEGFRIED
Loge – auf Felsen hoch ihr Sitz?

What scorches and sears
my feverish eyes?
Why lower those lids before mine?
Ha, fairest maid!
Keep your eyes closed!
My heart is aflame,
burnt by your glance.
Consuming torrents of fire
now boil my blood in my veins.
[with trembling voice]
Gunther, say, what shall I call her?

GUNTHER
Gutrune.

SIEGFRIED
And are they *good runes*
which I can read in her glances?
[he seizes Gutrune's hand]
To your brother offered I my
help;
his pride disdained my hand.
Will you, like him, deny me now,
or will you be my wife?
[Gutrune meets Hagen's glance, bows her
head and leaves the hall with a gesture
expressing her unworthiness]

SIEGFRIED
Have you, Gunther, a spouse?

GUNTHER
No wife have I.
The one I want
seems to elude my wish.
The one my heart desires,
she will never be my bride.

SIEGFRIED
Whom could you not wed,
with me to help?

GUNTHER
On soaring fell her home.

SIEGFRIED
On soaring fell her home?

In an unforgettable production by Wieland Wagner, Siegfried drank the potion from an outsize goblet which covered his face. When he lowered the vessel, Gutrune stood right in front of him, blotting out every other person and therewith every other memory.

Heinrich Porges, Wagner's assistant at the 1876 Bayreuth Festspiele, quotes the composer's remarks on 'the psychological aspect of the events symbolised (!) by the potion of forgetfulness'. The potion, Wagner seems to be saying, is not the actual cause of Siegfried's infatuation with Gutrune– it symbolizes Siegfried's readiness to forget Brünnhilde at the sight of Gutrune, and in so doing emphasizes the fickleness of the human heart.

Siegfried's mother Sieglinde once offered a welcoming drink to Siegmund, Siegfried's father. Sieglinde's and Gutrune's offerings both precipitate a *Liebestod*.

Wagner frequently paraphrases the irrational process of falling in love by the lovers' glance, as between Tristan and Isolde, Fasolt and Freia, Siegmund and Sieglinde, and now between Siegfried and Gutrune.

'Yesterday Siegfried drank Gutrune's fatal potion. I bet this will result in some calamity which I shall be forced to set to music.' (Wagner to Judith Gautier, 25 March 1870)

GUNTHER

Loge   Ein Feuer umbrennt den Saal –

SIEGFRIED

Loge   – ein Feuer umbrennt den Saal?

GUNTHER

Woodbird   Nur *wer* durch das Feuer bricht –

SIEGFRIED

– nur wer durch das Feuer bricht?

GUNTHER

Woodbird   *Amnesia*   – darf Brünnhildes Freier sein.

Nun darf ich den Fels nicht
   erklimmen;
das Feuer verglimmt mir nie!

SIEGFRIED

Loge   *Ich* fürchte kein Feuer,
für dich,frei ich die Frau:
denn dein Mann bin ich,
und mein Mut ist dein,
Gutrune   *Loge*   ge*winn* ich mir Gutrun zum *Weib.*

GUNTHER

Gutrune   *Loge*   *Gut*rune gönn ich dir gerne.

SIEGFRIED

Ride   *Loge*   *Brünnhil*de bring ich dir!

GUNTHER

Wie willst du sie täuschen?

SIEGFRIED

Loge   Durch des Tarnhelms Trug
tausch ich mir deine Gestalt.

GUNTHER

Loge   So stelle Eide zum Schwur!

SIEGFRIED

Bloodbrothers   *Blut*brüderschaft
Curse   *Treaty*   *Loge*   *Sword*   schwöre ein *Eid*!

GUNTHER
A fire surrounds the rock.

SIEGFRIED [astonished]
'A fire surrounds the rock' –

GUNTHER
But he who can brave the flames –

SIEGFRIED [trying very hard to
remember something]
'But he who can brave the flames' –

GUNTHER
– is Brünnhilde's conquering lord.
[at the mention of Brünnhilde's name
Siegfried reveals through a gesture that his
memory has deserted him]
I dare not set foot on the
    fellside;
the flames would not fade for me.

SIEGFRIED [comes to himself again from
his dream-like state]
I – fear not the fire.
The bride – she shall be yours;
for your man am I,
and my arm is yours,
if I can have Gutrun for wife.

GUNTHER
Gutrun I give you in marriage.

SIEGFRIED
Brünnhilde shall be yours.

GUNTHER
How will you deceive her?

SIEGFRIED
With my magic cap:
and I shall look like yourself.

GUNTHER
Then let an oath now be sworn!

SIEGFRIED
Bloodbrotherhood,
hallowed by oath!

Siegfried struggles desperately
against losing his memory. He
echoes Gunther's 'But he who can
brave the flames', as Wagner
directs, 'trying very hard to
remember.'

Earlier in this scene, Siegfried
pledged: 'This drink, Brünnhilde,
shall be yours!' Now he has fallen
for Gutrune and assigns his first
love to Gunther by the expedient
omission of a single comma:
'Brünnhilde shall be yours!'

In his first prose draft to
Siegfrieds Tod, Wagner explained
Siegfried's apparent treachery
with Siegfried saying to Gunther:
'As we change shapes, let us also
change our hearts and minds.'

Wagner's dramas are peopled
with bartered brides: Senta,
Isolde, Eva, now Gutrune, and
soon Brünnhilde.

<table>
<tr><td>*Gibichungen*</td><td>*Hagen*</td><td></td></tr>
<tr><td></td><td>*Treaty*</td><td></td></tr>
<tr><td></td><td>*Bloodbrothers*</td><td>*Blüh*enden Lebens
labendes Blut
träufelt ich *in den Trank*</td></tr>
<tr><td>*Gutrune*</td><td>*Loge*</td><td></td></tr>
</table>

GUNTHER

<table>
<tr><td>*Bloodbrothers*</td><td>*Bru*der-brünstig
mutig gemischt,</td></tr>
<tr><td>*Hagen*   *Treaty*</td><td>blüh im Trank unser *Blut*!</td></tr>
</table>

BEIDE

Bloodbrothers   *Treu*e trink ich dem Freund!

SIEGFRIED
Froh und frei –

GUNTHER
Froh und frei –

SIEGFRIED
– entblühe dem Bund –

GUNTHER
– entblühe dem Bund –

BEIDE

Treaty   Blutbrüderschaft *heut*.

GUNTHER

Atonement   *Bricht* ein Bruder den Bund:

SIEGFRIED

Atonement   Trügt den Treuen der Freund:

BEIDE

<table>
<tr><td>*Bloodbrothers*</td><td>Was in *Trop*fen heut
hold wir tranken,
in Strahlen ström es dahin,</td></tr>
<tr><td>*Curse*   *Treaty*</td><td>fromme Sühne dem *Freund*!</td></tr>
</table>

GUNTHER

Nothung   So biet ich den *Bund*!

[Hagen offers a drinking-horn, filled with
wine, to Gunther and Siegfried, who cut
their arms with their swords, holding them
over the horn which is still in Hagen's
hands]

Flourishing manhood's
freshening blood
into the drink I have dropped.

GUNTHER
Brother's brother
adds now his own:
blossom the drink by our blood!

BOTH
Faith I pledge to my friend.

SIEGFRIED
Joyous and free –

GUNTHER
Joyous and free –

SIEGFRIED
– shall bloom from our bond –

GUNTHER
– shall bloom from our bond –

BOTH
– bloodbrotherhood here!

GUNTHER
If a brother betrays –

SIEGFRIED
If a friend should be false –

BOTH
– what in drops today
we are drinking,
in torrents freely shall flow:
thus shall traitors atone!
[Gunther drinks and hands the horn to
Siegfried]

GUNTHER
So – blossom our bond!

Goethe's Faust makes over his
soul to Mephistopheles, who
demands his signature in blood:
'Blood it must be; blood has
peculiar virtues.'

Behind the innocuous artlessness
of this passage lurks danger. Wagner is fond of such celebratory,
strongly diatonic music when he
conceals hidden traps, as in the
Giants motif, Froh's rainbow
bridge, Wotan's giddy Walhall
vision and Gunther's welcome to
Siegfried.

To this same Atonement motif
Hunding had warned Siegfried's
father, Siegmund: 'Sacred is my
hearth, sacred hold you my
house!'

When the Tarnhelm is used to
confer invisibility, the wearer still
remains responsible for his own
actions. But when it is used to
change shapes, the wearer is no
longer in charge of his actions,
although he cannot escape the
consequences of any mis-
demeanour.

		SIEGFRIED
Bloodbrothers		So –
Nothung	*Treaty + Hagen*	trink ich dir *Treu.*
Bloodbrothers	*Gutrune*	

| *Atonement* | Was nahmst du am Eide nicht *teil?* |

HAGEN
Atonement — Mein Blut verdürb euch den
Trank;
Forge⌐ *nicht fliesst* mir's echt
Ring⌐ und edel wie euch:
störrisch und kalt
Forge stockt's in mir,
Liebe-Tragik nicht *will's* die Wange mir röten.
Drum bleib ich fern
Nothung vom feurigen *Bund.*

GUNTHER
Lass den unfrohen Mann!

SIEGFRIED
Hagen *Frisch* auf die Fahrt!
Loge⌐ *Ride*⌐ Dort liegt mein Schiff:
Tarnhelm schnell führt es zum Felsen.
Eine Nacht am Ufer
Hagen harrst du im Nachen;
die Frau fährst du dann heim.

GUNTHER
Loge⌐ Rastest du nicht zuvor?

SIEGFRIED
Um die Rückkehr ist's mir jach.

GUNTHER
Hagen *Loge* *Ride* Du, *Ha*gen! Bewache die Halle!

Hagen **GUTRUNE**
Wohin eilen die Schnellen?

SIEGFRIED
So –
flourish our faith!
[He drinks and passes the horn to Hagen,
who cuts it in two pieces with his sword.
Gunther and Siegfried join hands.]
[to Hagen]
Why did you not join in our oath?

HAGEN
My blood would blemish your
  drink.
Not pure and true
like yours will it flow.
Sluggish and cold,
slow to surge:
my cheek refuses to redden.
So I keep far
from fiery bonds.

GUNTHER
Let the sullen man be!

SIEGFRIED
Now on our way!
There lies my boat:
swift, sail to the mountain!
By the shore for one night
wait in the vessel,
and then bring home your bride!

GUNTHER
Would you not rest awhile?

SIEGFRIED
I am longing to return.

GUNTHER
You, Hagen, take charge of the
  palace!
[While they make for the shore, Hagen takes
up his spear and shield. Gutrune appears at
the door of her chamber.]

GUTRUNE
Such haste! What are they after?

Hagen shatters the drinking horn.
The custom still lives in the shat-
tering of glasses which have
served an important ceremony.

Hand in hand with the breaking-
up of treaties and promises goes
the breaking-up of matter in the
Ring: Siegmund's sword, Mime's
swords, Mime's anvil, Wotan's
spear, Brünnhilde's armour, the
World Ash Tree and the Norns'
rope of destiny.

			HAGEN
Hagen	*Ride*	*Loge*	Zu *Schiff* – *Brünn*hild zu frein.

	GUTRUNE
Loge	Siegfried?

HAGEN

Loge	Sieh, wie's ihn treibt
	zum Weib dich zu gewinnen.

	GUTRUNE
Hagen + Gutrune *Joy*	*Sieg*fried – mein!
Nibelungen Hate + Hagen	
Horn Call	

	HAGEN
Nibelungen Hate	Hier sitz ich zur Wacht,
	wahre den Hof,
	wehre die Halle dem Feind.
Grief *Gold's Dominion*	Gibichs Sohne
	wehet der Wind,
Hagen *Horn Call*	auf Werben fährt er dahin.
Siegfried	Ihm *führt das* Steuer
Grief *Gold's Dominion*	ein starker Held,
	Gefahr ihm will er bestehn:
Ride	die eigne Braut
	ihm bringt er zum Rhein;
Hagen + Liebe-Tragik *Rhinegold*	mir aber bringt er den *Ring*!
	Ihr freien Söhne,
	frohe Gesellen,
Liebe-Tragik	*se*gelt nur lustig dahin:
	dünkt er euch niedrig,
Walhall *Rhinegold*	ihr *dient* ihm doch,
	des Niblungen Sohn.

HAGEN
To bring Brünnhilde here.

GUTRUNE
Siegfried?

HAGEN [seats himself slowly in front of
the hall]
See how he speeds,
to sail back and to woo you.

GUTRUNE
Siegfried – mine!
[Greatly agitated, Gutrune returns to her
chamber. Hagen sits motionless, leaning his
back against the doorpost at the entrance to
the hall.]

In allowing herself to be manipulated by Hagen, Gutrune becomes a pathetic accessory to a
pathetic mismatch.

HAGEN
Here sit I on guard,
watching the house,
warding the hall from the foe.
Gibich's son
speeds with the wind;
he sails in search of a wife.
His helm is held
by a mighty man,
who outdares danger for him.
His rightful bride
he'll bring to the Rhine,
and he will bring me – the ring!
You sons of freedom,
carefree companions,
sail on your jubilant way!
Though you despise me,
you all shall serve
the Nibelung's son!

'The orchestra in Hagen's watch
sounds as though the instruments
were strung with the plumage of
ravens.' (Cosima to Nietzsche, 15
May 1875)

The battle between Wotan and
Alberich has shifted to their off-
spring, Siegfried and Hagen.

I. Akt: 3. Szene

BRÜNNHILDE
Altgewohntes Geräusch
Ride raunt meinem Ohr die Ferne.
Ein Luftross jagt
im Laufe daher;
auf der Wolke fährt es
wetternd zum Fels.
Wer fand mich Einsame auf?

WALTRAUTES STIMME
Valkyrie Cry Brünnhil*de*! *Schwe*ster!
Schläfst oder wachst du?

BRÜNNHILDE
Valkyrie Cry Waltrautes Ruf, so wonnig mir
kund!
Kommst du Schwester?
Schwingst dich kühn zu mir her?
Dort im Tann
– dir noch vertraut –
steige vom Ross
und stell den Renner zur Rast!

Kommst du zu mir?
Bist du so kühn,
magst ohne Grauen
Death Brünnhild bieten den Gruss?

WALTRAUTE
Einzig dir nur
galt meine Eil.

BRÜNNHILDE
So wagtest du, Brünnhild zulieb,

Act I: Scene 3

[Brünnhilde sits at the entrance of the cave,
contemplating Siegfried's ring. Distant thunder and lightning. A dark thundercloud
approaches the rock.]

BRÜNNHILDE
Sounds, familiar of old,
steal from afar upon me.
It is a steed,
comes winging this way.
On the clouds it flies
in storm to the fell.
Who haunts Brünnhilde's repose?

WALTRAUTE'S VOICE
Brünnhilde! Sister!
Wake if you slumber!

BRÜNNHILDE
Waltraute's call! How welcome the
      sound!
Fearless sister,
boldly flying to me.
By those trees,
still dear to you,
light from your horse;
allow the courser to rest.
[she hastens towards her, then returns with
her sister]
So you have come.
O, you are brave,
daring to seek out
Brünnhild's lonely retreat.

WALTRAUTE
For your sake
my feverish haste!

BRÜNNHILDE
Your care for me, Brünnhild, your kin,

One of Wagner's masterstrokes:
Brünnhilde's reverie, as she contemplates the ring and all it
stands for, is portrayed by two
clarinets, meandering in parallel
thirds, trilling and reminiscing to
the Liebesglück motif.

Walvaters Bann zu brechen?
Oder wie – o sag! –
wär wider mich Wotans Sinn
   erweicht?
Als dem Gott entgegen
Siegmund ich schützte,
fehlend – ich weiss es –
Death   erfüllt ich doch *seinen* Wunsch.
Dass sein Zorn sich verzogen,
weiss ich auch.
Denn verschloss er mich gleich in
   Schlaf,
fesselt' er mich auf dem Fels,
Grief   wies er dem Mann mich zur *Magd*
Wotan's Child   der am Weg mich fänd und erweckt

meiner bangen Bitte
doch gab er Gunst:
Ride   *Loge*   mit *zehren*dem *Feuer*
umzog er den Fels,
Wotan's Child   dem Zagen zu wehren den Weg.
So zur Seligsten
Hosanna   schuf mich die Strafe:
Siegfried   *der* herrlichste Held
gewann mich zum Weib!
In seiner Liebe
Hosanna   *Valkyrie Cry*   leucht und lach ich heut *auf*!
Lockte dich Schwester mein
   Los?
An meiner Wonne
willst du dich weiden,
teilen, was mich betraf?

WALTRAUTE
Teilen den Taumel,
der dich Törin erfasst?
Ein Andres bewog mich in Angst,
zu brechen Wotans Gebot.

BRÜNNHILDE
Angst und Furcht
fesseln dich Arme?
So verzieh der Strenge noch nicht?
Wotan's Frustration   Du zagst vor des Strafenden Zorn?

WALTRAUTE
Dürft ich ihn fürchten,
meiner Angst fänd ich ein End!

made you defy our father?
Or perhaps – o say!
has he at last, has he softened his
    heart?
When, against the godhead,
Siegmund I guarded,
flouting his words,
I kept faith with his innermost will.
Now his anger is ended,
I am sure.
For although I was locked in
    sleep,
fettered alone on the fell,
proffered as prize to the man
who should wake and win me for
    wife:
I appealed for pity –
he granted grace.
With furious flames
he encircled the rock,
to frighten the fearful away.
Thus, great fortune
arose from affliction:
a wonderful hero
won me as wife.
Blest in his love,
I live in laughter and light.
Has this my bliss brought you
    here?
And would you, sister,
feast on my fortune,
sharing these joys of mine?

WALTRAUTE
Sharing the madness
that has muddled your mind?
In dread and dismay have I come,
disdaining Wotan's decree.

BRÜNNHILDE
Why such fear,
faint-hearted sister?
But I see, he will not forgive.
You, too, are afraid of his wrath.

WALTRAUTE
Could I but fear him,
at an end were all my fear.

Brünnhilde's fate parallels that of
Prometheus: both were fettered
to a rock by a god.

Prometheus says to Hermes (sent
by Zeus): 'Have you come to this
peak to gaze at my torment? ...
Are you here to gaze at what I
suffer and add your grief to
mine?' (Aeschylus: *Prometheus
Bound*)

BRÜNNHILDE
Staunend versteh ich dich nicht.

WALTRAUTE
Wehre der Wallung,
achtsam höre mich an!
Nach Walhall wieder
treibt mich die Angst,
die von Walhall hierher mich trieb.

BRÜNNHILDE
Wotan's Frustration — Was ist's mit den ewigen Göttern?

WALTRAUTE
Wotan's Frustration — Höre mit Sinn, was ich dir sage!
Seit er von dir geschieden,
zur Schlacht nicht mehr
Wotan's Frustration — schickte uns Wotan:
irr und ratlos
ritten wir ängstlich zu Heer;
Wotan's Frustration **Revenge** — *Walhalls* mutige *Hel*den
Erda — mied Walvater.
Einsam zu Ross,
ohne Ruh noch Rast,
Walhall — durchschweift er als Wandrer die
Crisis — Welt.
Treaty — Jüngst kehrte er heim;
in der Hand hielt er
Walhall — seines *Spee*res Splitter,
Crisis — die hatte ein Held ihm geschlagen.
Mit stummem Wink
Walhalls Edle
wies er zum Forst,
Walhall · Crisis · Authority — die Weltesche zu fällen.
Des Stammes Scheite
hiess er sie schichten
zu ragendem Hauf
Walhall — rings um der Seligen *Saal.*
Der Götter Rat
liess er berufen;
den Hochsitz nahm
Götterdämmerung · Walhall — *hei*lig er ein:
ihm zu Seiten
hiess er die Bangen sich setzen,
in Ring und Reih
Crisis — die Hall erfüllen die Helden.
Fate · Walhall — So sitzt er,
Crisis — sagt kein Wort,
Fate · Crisis — auf hehrem *Sit*ze

BRÜNNHILDE
How can I fathom your words?

WALTRAUTE
Calm your disquiet,
and attend to me now.
To Walhall terror
urges me back,
that from Walhall urged me to you.

BRÜNNHILDE [alarmed]
What fortune awaits the eternals?

WALTRAUTE
Listen with care, and I will tell you.
Since you and he were sundered,
we waged no more
warfare for Wotan.
All bewildered
rode we in fear to the field.
Walhall's valiant heroes –
Wotan shunned them.
Riding alone,
without peace or pause,
as Wanderer he roamed through
   the world.
At last he came home.
In his hand held he
his great spear in splinters.
A hero had hacked it asunder.
With silent sign,
Walhall's heroes
charged he to cut
the World Ash Tree to pieces.
The mighty boughs
they gathered and bundled,
then piled them up high,
circling the hall of the blest.
The holy host
Wotan then rallied,
and sat himself
high on his throne.
By his side
he gathered an anxious assembly;
around him thronged
the ample array of his heroes.
So sits he,
speaks no word,
enthroned and lordly,

Apart from its dramatic con-
sequence, this scene serves the
useful function of telling us of
recent events in Walhall.

Motif	Text
(Crisis)	stumm und ernst,
	des Speeres Splitter
Crisis — *Golden Apples*	fest in der Faust;
	Holdas Äpfel
	rührt er nicht an.
Walhall	*Staunen* und Bangen
Crisis — *Crisis* — *Grief*	bin*den* starr die Götter.
	Seine Raben beide
	sandt er auf Reise;
	kehrten die einst
	mit guter Kunde zurück,
Joy	dann noch *ein*mal,
	– zum letzten Mal! –
Wotan's Frustration	lächelte ewig der Gott.
	Seine Knie umwindend
	liegen wir Walküren;
	blind bleibt er
	den flehenden Blicken:
	uns alle verzehrt
Wotan's Frustration	Zagen und endlose Angst.
Revenge	An seine *Brust*
	presst ich mich weinend;
Wotan's Farewell	da *brach* sich sein Blick;
	er gedachte, Brünnhilde, dein.
	Tief seufzt er auf,
	schloss das Auge,
	und wie im Traume
	raunt er das Wort:
	'Des tiefen Rheines Töchtern
Liebe-Tragik — *Curse*	gäbe den *Ring* sie *wieder*
	zurück,
Joy	von des Fluches Last
Walhall	er*löst* wär Gott und Welt!'
Wotan's Frustration	Da sann ich nach:
Revenge	*von* seiner Seite
	durch stumme Reihen
Wotan's Frustration	stahl ich *mich* fort;
Revenge	in heimlicher *Hast*
	bestieg ich mein Ross,
Ride	*und* ritt im Sturme zu dir.
	Dich, o Schwester,
	beschwör ich nun:
	was du vermagst,
	vollend es dein Mut;
Wotan's Frustration	ende der Ewigen Qual!

BRÜNNHILDE
Welch banger Träume Mären

stern and still,
the splintered spear
held fast in his hand.
Holda's apples
will he not taste.
Heavy and heart-sick
sit the gods in silence.
He has sent his ravens
out on an errand.
Should they return
with happy tidings to him,
then once more,
and then nevermore
Wotan, our father, would smile.
Round his knees, in terror,
tremble the Valkyries.
He heeds not
our silent entreaty.
We all are afraid,
harrowed with endless alarm.
I flung myself,
weeping, on Wotan's breast;
then soft grew his gaze:
in his heart was Brünnhild alone.
Our father sighed.
With his eye closed,
as in a dream,
he whispered these words:
'If but the Rhine's fair daughters
gathered the ring from Brünnhilde's
   hand,
then the curse dissolves,
and saved were god and world.'
I thought on this,
and then I left him;
through silent circles
stole I away.
In secretive haste
I mounted my steed,
and rode at once to your rock.
Now, my sister,
I beg of you:
what you can do,
that dare do today!
Rescue the gods from their doom!
[she throws herself at Brünnhilde's feet]

BRÜNNHILDE
What dream-born, crazy tale

Waltraute is now what Brünnhilde
once was. Her care is for the
gods, Brünnhilde's is for Siegfried.

meldest du Traurige mir!
Der *Göt*ter heiligem
Himmelsnebel
bin ich Törin enttaucht;

nicht fass ich, was ich erfahre.
Wirr und wüst
scheint mir dein Sinn:
in deinem Aug,
so übermüde,
glänzt flackernde Glut.
Mit blasser Wange,
du bleiche Schwester,

was willst du Wilde von *mir*?

WALTRAUTE
An deiner Hand, der Ring -
er ist's; hör meinen Rat:
für Wotan wirf ihn von dir!

BRÜNNHILDE
Den Ring – von mir?

WALTRAUTE
Den Rheintöchtern gib ihn zurück!

BRÜNNHILDE

Den Rheintöchtern – ich – den *Ring*?
Siegfrieds Liebespfand!
Bist du von Sinnen?

WALTRAUTE
Hör mich, hör meine Angst!

Der Welt *Un*heil
haftet sicher an ihm.
Wirf ihn von dir,
fort in die Welle,
Walhalls Elend zu enden,

den verfluchten wirf in die Flut!

BRÜNNHILDE
Ha! weisst du, was er mir ist?
Wie kannst du's fassen,

fühllose Maid!
Mehr als Walhalls Wonne,
mehr als der Ewigen Ruhm
ist mir der Ring:
ein Blick auf sein helles Gold,
ein Blitz aus dem hehren Glanz

you carry, sad sister, to me!
The gods' and Walhall's
hazy glory
have I long left behind.
No meaning has your message.
Wild and strange
seem all your words;
and in your eyes,
so sorrow-laden,
gleam flickering fires.
Your face is ashen,
unhappy sister.
But what would you have me do?

WALTRAUTE [vehemently]
The ring upon your hand,
that ring! listen to me:
for Wotan, let the ring go!

BRÜNNHILDE
Let go my ring?

WALTRAUTE
The Rhinemaidens must have their
    own!

BRÜNNHILDE
The Rhinemaidens? I? The ring?
Siegfried's pledge of love!
Are you demented?

WALTRAUTE
Hear me! See my distress!
The world's doomsday
surely lurks in that ring.
O return it,
back to the waters!
Walhall's woe must be ended:
cast the hateful ring in the Rhine!

BRÜNNHILDE
Learn what this ring means to me.
Can you not fathom,
unfeeling maid:
more than Walhall's pleasures,
more than the pomp of the gods,
more is this ring.
One glance at its golden blaze,
one flash from its noble fire

The scene presents an escape
clause: were Brünnhilde to heed
her sister's plea, she might yet
avert the impending disaster that
threatens herself and the world.

Brünnhilde misreads the symbol.
The ring stands for Power; but to
her it represents Love.

Bequest

gilt mir werter
als aller Götter
ewig währendes *Glück*.
Denn selig aus ihm

Brünnhilde leuchtet mir Siegfrieds Liebe, –
Siegfrieds Liebe!
O, liess sich die Wonne dir

Hosanna sagen!

Wotan's Frustration *Revenge* Sie wahrt mir der Reif.
Geh hin zu der Götter

Wotan's Frustration heiligem Rat!
Von meinem Ringe
raune ihnen zu:

Liebe-Tragik die *Lie*be liesse ich nie,

Walhall mir nähmen nie sie die Liebe,
stürzt auch in Trümmern

Wotan's Frustration Walhalls strahlende Pracht!

WALTRAUTE

Curse Dies deine *Treue*?
So in Trauer

Wotan's Frustration entlässest du lieblos die Schwe*ster*?

BRÜNNHILDE

Curse Schwinge dich fort,
fliehe zu Ross!
Den Reif entführst du mir nie!

WALTRAUTE

Grief *We*he! Wehe!
Weh dir, Schwester!

Loge *Valkyrie Cry* *Ride* Walhalls Göttern weh!

BRÜNNHILDE

Ride Blitzend Gewölk,
vom Wind getragen,
stürme dahin:

Magic Fire zu mir nie steure mehr her!

Abendlich Dämmern
deckt den Himmel;
heller leuchtet

Loge die hütende Lohe herauf.

I prize dearer
than the eternals'
everlasting delight.
This glittering gold
tells me that Siegfried loves me.
Siegfried loves me!
O could you but learn what this
   love is!
Love lives in this ring.
Then go to the holy
host of the gods,
and of my ring
report Brünnhilde's words:
my love shall outlast my life,
nor shall I ever renounce it.
Sooner be shattered
Walhall's glorious show!

WALTRAUTE
Brünnhilde faithless!
To her sorrow
you really abandon your sister?

BRÜNNHILDE
Fly on your way!
Swiftly to horse!
The ring is mine while I live!

WALTRAUTE
Rack and ruin!
Weep, my sister!
Doomed is Walhall! Woe!
[She rushes away. A thundercloud rises
from the forest.]

BRÜNNHILDE
[watches the vanishing cloud]
Thunder and storm clouds,
borne by the wind –
now wing your way home,
and no more voyage this way!
[It is evening. The light from the fire below
increases.]
Evening shadows
shroud the heavens.
Bravely blazes
the guardian fire below.
[ever brighter tongues of flame dart over
the edge of the rock]

Brünnhilde's divine recklessness
mirrors that of Siegmund in Act II
of *Walküre*: 'My greetings to Walhall ... I shall not follow you
there!'

(Loge)		Was leckt so wütend
		die lodernde Welle zum Wall?
		Zur Felsenspitze
	Siegfried	wälzt sich der feurige Schwall.

Magic Fire + Horn Call		Siegfried!
Liebe-Tragik		*Sieg*fried zurück!
Horn Call		Seinen Ruf sendet er *her*!
		Auf! Auf! Ihm entgegen!
Siegfried	*Horn Call*	In mei*nes* Gottes *Arm*!

Hagen	*Tarnhelm*	Verrat! Wer drang zu mir?
	Gibichungen	
		SIEGFRIED

Hagen + Tarnhelm		*Brünn*hild! Ein Freier kam,
Tarnhelm	*Amnesia*	den dein Feuer nicht ge*schreckt*.
	Gibichungen	Dich werb ich nun zum Weib:
		du folge willig mir!
		BRÜNNHILDE
	Curse	Wer ist *der* Mann
		der das vermochte,
	Tarnhelm	was dem *Stärk*sten nur bestimmt?
Amnesia		SIEGFRIED
	Gibichungen	Ein Held, der dich zähmt,
		bezwingt Gewalt dich nur.
		BRÜNNHILDE
		Ein Unhold schwang sich
	Grief	auf jenen *Stein*.
		Ein Aar kam geflogen,
		mich zu zerfleischen!
Hagen	*Tarnhelm*	Wer bist du, *Schreck*licher?
		Stammst du von Menschen?
		Kommst du von Hellas
	Amnesia	nächtlichem *Heer*?

It leaps up madly,
and now it will mount to the sky.
My mountain peak
burns bright in the fiery flood.
[Siegfried's horn sounds from below.
Brünnhilde starts up in delight.]
Siegfried!
Siegfried is here,
and his call comforts my heart.
Up! Up! I must meet him!
Now for my god's embrace!
[Siegfried leaps forward, out of the flames
which immediately begin to recede. The
Tarnhelm hides Siegfried's face, except
his eyes; it causes him to look like
Gunther.]
Betrayed! Who braved the flames?

SIEGFRIED [leaning on his shield,
contemplating Brünnhilde in silence;
he addresses her in a feigned voice, deeper
than his own]
Brünnhild! A suitor came,
whom your fire does not scare.
I want you as my wife:
say yes and follow me!

BRÜNNHILDE
Who is the man
who would endeavour
what the strongest may not dare?

SIEGFRIED
A hero holds you fast,
if force alone avails.

BRÜNNHILDE [seized with horror]
A fiend has found me
here on the fell.
An eagle has landed,
to tear me to pieces.
Who are you, dreadful one?
Are you a mortal?
Are you of Hella's
dark, dismal host?

Who is it that calls 'Brünnhild!'?
Siegfried, or Gunther? The orchestra proclaims a double motif:
Tarnhelm with Hagen. This reveals
that whoever the caller may be,
he is being manipulated by
Hagen.

Siegfried, disguised by the Tarnhelm, looks and acts like the con-
temptible Gunther. The Tarnhelm
motif itself seems petrified by its
own callous success: each chord
takes four bars, the music sharing
in Brünnhilde's horror.

An eagle, according to Aeschylus,
was sent by Zeus to pounce upon
Prometheus.

Act I, Scene 3: Libretto   85

SIEGFRIED

Gibichungen

Ein Gibichung bin ich,
und Gunther heisst der *Held*,
dem, Frau, du folgen sollst!

BRÜNNHILDE
Wotan! Ergrimmter,
grausamer Gott!
Weh! Nun erseh ich
Revenge   der Strafe Sinn.
Zu Hohn und Jammer
Hagen   Crisis   Hagen   Nibelungen Hate   jagst du mich *hin!*

SIEGFRIED
Amnesia   Die Nacht bricht an,
in deinem Gemach
musst du dich mir vermählen!

BRÜNNHILDE

Ring   Bleib fern! Fürchte dies Zeichen!
Grief   Zur Schande zwingst du mich *nicht,*
Gold's Dominion   so lang der Ring mich be*schützt.*

SIEGFRIED
Hagen   *Man*nesrecht gebe er Gunther.
Durch den Ring sei ihm vermählt!

BRÜNNHILDE
Zurück, du Räuber!
Frevelnder Dieb!
Gold's Dominion   Erfreche dich nicht, mir zu *nahn!*
Stärker als Stahl
macht mich der Ring:
Curse   nie raubst du ihn mir!

SIEGFRIED
Von dir ihn zu lösen,
Grief   Ride   Consorts   lehrst du mich nun.
Curse   Hagen   Ride
Curse   Liebesglück
Brünnhilde   Tarnhelm

Amnesia   Jetzt bist du *mein,*
Nibelungen Hate   Brünnhilde, Gunthers Braut.
Nibelungen Hate   Brünnhilde   Gönne mir nun dein Gemach!

SIEGFRIED
[beginning with a slightly trembling voice,
but then firmly]
A Gibichung am I,
and Gunther is my name.
Now come and follow me!

BRÜNNHILDE
Wotan, you ruthless,
rigorous god!
Woe, now I fathom
my punishment!
Disgraced am I,
an object of scorn.

SIEGFRIED
The night has come,
and here where you live,
you must be mine in marriage!

BRÜNNHILDE [stretching out the finger
with Siegfried's ring]
Stand back! Bow to this token!
Its power shields me from shame.
This golden ring is my guard.

SIEGFRIED
Husband's right gives it to Gunther.
Let the ring make you his wife.

BRÜNNHILDE
Away, you robber!
Villainous thief!
Nor, miscreant, dare to advance!
Stronger than steel
makes me this ring.
Fiend! here you must fail!

SIEGFRIED
To ravish the ring
I learn from your lips.
[They struggle. She flees, he pursues. After a
violent struggle he draws the ring from her
finger. She shrieks, sinks into his arms, and
her eyes meet Siegfried's.]
Now you are mine,
Brünnhilde, Gunther's bride.
Come, share your chamber with me!

When Siegfried announces himself as 'a Gibichung' Wagner
grants him a residual trace of
decency: he directs Siegfried to
sing with 'a somewhat trembling
voice'.

With hindsight, the tender Woodbird in *Siegfried* can be seen as
Siegfried's evil genius. It advised
him to win 'the Tarnhelm whose
magic shall bring great love and
renown'.

A degrading spectacle. The potion
not only makes Siegfried forget
the past. It makes him forget
himself.

Wotan once ripped the ring from
Alberich's finger. His grandson
Siegfried now repeats the despic-
able deed, but this time from
Brünnhilde's finger.

Nibelungen Hate		*Brünnhilde*	

BRÜNNHILDE

Was könntest du wehren,
elendes Weib!

Nibelungen Hate		*Hagen*	*Revenge*
Nothung	*Sword*	*Hagen*	*Treaty*

SIEGFRIED

	Liebe-Tragik
	Gutrune

Nun, *N*othung, zeuge du,
dass ich in Züchten *warb*.
Die Treue wahrend dem Bruder,
trenne mich von seiner *Braut*!

Sword	*Nothung*
Tarnhelm	*Amnesia*
	Nothung

	Brünnhilde
	Tarnhelm

BRÜNNHILDE [exhausted, stares
before her]
Defenceless and helpless,
ill-fated wife!

SIEGFRIED [drives her on towards her
cave, then draws his sword]
Now, Nothung, speak for me,
that I have chastely wooed.
To keep my pledge to my brother,
part me from my brother's bride!
[He follows Brünnhilde. The curtain falls.]

Having been abandoned by
Wotan, her adored father,
Brünnhilde is again abandoned,
this time by her beloved Siegfried,
whose eyes the Tarnhelm could
not disguise.

Friedrich Dalberg as Hagen in
the 1942 production at Bayreuth

II
Act

Synopsis
Leitmotifs
Libretto

Act II: Story

Outside the Gibichung Hall

Scene 1
Alberich appears to Hagen and urges him to regain the ring.
Alberich vanishes.

Scene 2
Siegfried arrives and tells Hagen of the imminent arrival of Gunther and Brünnhilde. Gutrune questions Siegfried about his con-
quest of Brünnhilde and wonders whether her new husband has
remained faithful to her.

Scene 3
Hagen summons the Gibichung vassals to welcome Gunther and his new bride, Brünnhilde.

Scene 4
When Brünnhilde sees Siegfried at Gutrune's side she is puzzled and mortified. Noticing the ring on Siegfried's finger, however, she is convinced of Siegfried's treachery and infidelity. Hagen persuades Gunther that Siegfried has broken his oath, when he conquered and slept with his bloodbrother's new wife. Siegfried is too confused to grasp the meaning of Brünnhilde's wrath. Both he and Brünnhilde swear an oath, protesting their own integrity.

Scene 5
Hagen, Gunther and Brünnhilde plot Siegfried's death.

Act II: Action

1. Orchestra: Prelude
2. Alberich appears to Hagen
3. Orchestra: Dawn
4. Siegfried's arrival
5. Hagen summons the vassals
6. Gunther presents Brünnhilde to his court
7. Brünnhilde's distress
8. Brünnhilde's and Siegfried's oath
9. Siegfried's unwarranted high spirits
10. Hagen, Gunther and Brünnhilde decide on Siegfried's death

Hagen (Josef Greindl) summons the vassals; photograph of a Bayreuth production of the 1950s

Act II: Leitmotif

Only one leitmotif is new to this act. It is given below, together with the page number of first appearance.

Murder p.98

The final leitmotif of the cycle first appears, fittingly, at the nocturnal meeting of Alberich and Hagen. It is chromatically warped and harmonically grating. If it was Wagner's intention to present sheer evil in musical terms, he has ghoulishly succeeded.

II. Akt: 1. Szene

ALBERICH

Nibelungen Hate⌉   *Schläfst* du, Hagen, mein Sohn?
Du schläfst und hörst mich nicht,
den Ruh und Schlaf verriet?

HAGEN

Ich höre dich, schlimmer Albe:

Grief   *Ring*   was hast du meinem Schlaf zu
sagen?

ALBERICH
Gemahnt sei der Macht,
der du gebietest,
bist du so mutig,

Nibelungen Hate⌉   *Liebe-Tragik*   wie die *Mut*ter dich mir gebar!

HAGEN
Gab mir die Mutter Mut,
nicht mag ich ihr doch danken,
dass deiner List sie erlag:
frühalt, fahl und bleich,

Liebe-Tragik   hass ich die Frohen,
freue mich nie.

ALBERICH
Hagen, mein Sohn!
Hasse die Frohen!
Mich Lustfreien,
Leidbelasteten
liebst du so, wie du sollst!
Bist du kräftig,
kühn und klug:
die wir bekämpfen
mit nächtigem Krieg,

Act II: Scene 1

[Open space by the river bank, outside Gunther's hall. Altar-stones to Wotan,
Fricka and Donner. Night. Hagen sits
sleeping, Alberich crouching before him.]

ALBERICH
Hear me, Hagen, my son!
You sleep and hear not him
who cannot find repose.

HAGEN [motionless, sleeping with
open eyes]
I mark your words, cunning
    Niblung.
What must your sleeping son
    remember?

ALBERICH
Remember your strength:
it is your substance.
Are you as manly
as your mother meant you to be?

HAGEN
My courage comes from her,
and yet I cannot thank her
that she succumbed to your craft.
Gaunt, grey, early old,
hating the happy,
stranger to joy.

ALBERICH
Hagen, my son,
hate what is happy!
Deprived am I,
sorrow-laden;
I deserve all your love.
Now be fearless,
fail me not!
Those whom with murderous
craft we defy,

A very high C flat on flute and
oboe coincides with the sudden
shaft of moonlight that reveals
the sleeping Hagen.

In the nocturnal meeting of
Alberich and Hagen, myth meets
history.

The timbre of the low strings and
brass, the syncopation, and the
motifs (Nibelungen Hate, Hagen
and Grief) all combine to give this
muted orchestral prelude an
other-worldly aspect, as befits the
ensuing meeting of Alberich and
Hagen, gloomy father and gloomy
son. The music portrays a world
without love, laughter or hope.

Mirroring Wotan's decline from
chief god to wandering observer,
Alberich has taken to loitering
and snooping, first around Fafner's cave, and now by the
portals of the Gibichung hall.

Alberich calls Hagen by his name
not once but seven times.
'Schlimmer Albe' ('cunning
Niblung') is Hagen's sole and
rather unfilial acknowledgment of
his relationship to his father.

		Ring	schon gibt ihnen Not unser Neid.
			Der einst den Ring mir entriss,
		Nibelungen Hate	Wotan, der wütende Räuber,
			vom eignen Geschlechte
			ward er geschlagen:
		Sword	an *den* Wälsung verlor er
		Walhall	Macht und Ge*walt*;
			mit der Götter ganzer Sippe
		Nibelungen Hate	in Angst ersieht er sein *En*de.
			Nicht ihn fürcht ich mehr:
			fallen muss er mit allen!
	Hagen	*Nibelungen Hate*	Schläfst du, Hagen, mein Sohn?

HAGEN

		Nibelungen Hate	Der Ewigen Macht,
		Murder	wer erbte sie?

ALBERICH
Ich – und du!
Wir erben die Welt.
Trüg ich mich nicht
in deiner Treu,
teilst du meinen Gram und Grimm.

		Sword + Siegfried	*Wotans* Speer
		Treaty	zerspellte der *Wälsung*,
		Fafner	der *Faf*ner, den Wurm,
			im Kampfe gefällt
			und kindisch den Reif sich errang.
		Ring	Jede Ge*walt*
			hat er gewonnen;
			Walhall und Nibelheim
			neigen sich ihm.
			An dem furchtlosen Helden
			erlahmt selbst mein Fluch:
			denn nicht kennt er
			des Ringes Wert,
			zu nichts nützt er
		Horn Call	die neidlichste *Macht*.
			Lachend in liebender Brunst,
			brennt er lebend dahin.
		Hagen	Ihn zu ver*der*ben,
	Liebe-Tragik	*Nibelungen Hate*	taugt uns nun *einz*ig!
			Hörst du, Hagen, mein Sohn?

HAGEN

Hagen	*Nibelungen Hate*	*Hagen*	Zu seinem Ver*der*ben
		Murder	dient er mir schon.

shall soon be the slaves of our spite.
And he who captured the ring,
Wotan, that ruthless robber:
his very own brood
has broken his power.
To the Wälsung has passed
dominion and might.
With his tribe of gods around him,
in dread he waits for his downfall.
I fear him no more.
He must fall when they all fall.
Hear me, Hagen, my son!

HAGEN
The might of the gods,
who wins it all?

ALBERICH
I – and you!
The world will be ours,
can I but trust
in Hagen's troth.
Yours is all my pride and pain.
Wotan's spear
was split by the Wälsung,
and Fafner the dragon
fell to his sword.
The ring was the boy's reward.
His is the gain,
his is the glory.
Walhall and Nibelheim
kneel to their lord,
and this unfearing hero
my curse cannot harm;
for he knows not
the ring's repute,
nor makes use
of its magical might.
Laughter and love are his all,
burning up life as he lives.
Siegfried must perish:
this is our purpose.
Hear me, Hagen, my son!

HAGEN
His doom is already
destined by me.

Alberich manipulates his son
Hagen. In *Walküre*, Wotan manipulated his son Siegmund.

			ALBERICH
			Den goldnen Ring,
		Wotan's Child	den Reif gilt's zu erringen!
		Wälsungen	*Ein* weises Weib
		Nibelungen Hate	lebt dem Wälsung zu *lieb*:
			riet es ihm je
			des Rheines Töchtern,
			die in Wassers Tiefen
			einst mich betört,
		Ring	*zurück*zugeben den Ring,
			verloren ging' mir das Gold,
			keine List erlangte es je.
		Murder	*Drum* ohne Zögern
			ziel auf den Reif!
		Nibelungen Hate	Dich *Zag*losen
			zeugt ich mir ja,
			dass wider Helden
			hart du mir hieltest.
Nibelungen Hate	*Fafner*		Zwar *stark* nicht genug,
	Fafner	*Sword*	den Wurm zu bestehn,
			was allein dem Wälsung bestimmt,
		Murder	zu zähem Hass doch
			erzog ich Hagen;
			der soll mich nun rächen,
			den Ring gewinnen
			dem Wälsung und Wotan zum
		Walhall	*Hohn*!
			Schwörst du mir's, Hagen, mein
		Nibelungen Hate	Sohn?
			HAGEN
		Nibelungen Hate	Den Ring soll ich haben:
			harre in Ruh!
			ALBERICH
			Schwörst du mir's, Hagen, mein
		Nibelungen Hate	Held?
			HAGEN
	Nibelungen Hate	*Curse*	Mir selbst schwör ich's;
			schweige die Sorge!
			ALBERICH
		Grief	*Sei* treu, Hagen, mein Sohn!
			Trauter Helde! Sei treu!
			Sei treu! Treu!

ALBERICH
The golden ring,
that ring must be recaptured!
O she is wise,
she who lives by his love.
Prompted by her,
the Rhine's fair daughters
– who in watery deeps
befooled me before –
might have the ring from his hand.
That golden ring would be gone,
and no guile could win it again.
Do not delay,
but hunt for the ring!
A stranger to fear
you were bred,
that against heroes
your hand might help me.
Not potent enough
for Fafner the fiend,
who to none but Siegfried could
    fall:
to deadly hatred
I brought up Hagen.
My son will avenge me,
the ring he'll win me.
See Wälsung and Wotan
    undone!
Swear to me, Hagen, my son!

HAGEN
The ring shall be ravished:
rest and repose!

ALBERICH
Swear to me, Hagen, my pride!

HAGEN
My will swears it;
silence your sorrow!

ALBERICH [disappearing, his voice
sounding fainter]
Be true, Hagen, my son!
Trusty hero, be true!
Be true! True!
[Hagen, now alone, still in the same position,
gazes towards the Rhine which begins to
glow in the light of dawn]

This scene also serves as an aid to
memory, as Alberich recapitulates
Wotan's winning of the ring,
Siegfried's slaying of Fafner and
his love for Brünnhilde, and the
Rhinemaidens' longing for the
ring's return.

Hagen's promises, 'The ring shall
be ravished' and 'My will swears
it', cannot reassure Alberich, who
admonishes his son four times to
'be true', before fading away.

Was this a real dialogue, a ghostly
visitation or a dream? And if it
was a dream, whose dream was
it, Hagen's or Alberich's?

II. Akt: 2. Szene

SIEGFRIED
Hoiho, Hagen!
Müder Mann!
Siehst du mich kommen?

HAGEN
Loge   Hei, Siegfried!
Geschwinder Helde!
Wo brausest du *her*?

SIEGFRIED
Loge   Vom Brünnhildenstein!
Dort sog ich den Atem ein,
mit dem ich dich rief:
Horn Call   so *rasch* war meine Fahrt!
Langsamer folgt mir ein Paar:
zu Schiff gelangt das her!

HAGEN
So zwangst du Brünnhild?

SIEGFRIED
Gutrune   Wacht Gutrune?

HAGEN
Gutrune   Hoiho, Gutrune,
komm heraus!
Loge   *Sieg*fried ist da:
was säumst du drin?

SIEGFRIED
Loge   Euch beiden meld ich,
Gutrune   wie ich Brünnhild band.
Heiss mich willkommen,
Gibichkind!
Gutrune   Ein guter Bote bin ich *dir*.

A bass clarinet introduces this
morning music, which is then
solemnly presented by eight
horns, entering one after another.
Towards its end they are joined
by bassoons, trombones and low
strings.

Act II: Scene 2

[Hagen wakes with a start as Siegfried
suddenly appears in his own shape, but with
the Tarnhelm on his head. Siegfried takes it
off as he approaches Hagen.]

SIEGFRIED
Hoiho! Hagen!
Weary man!
Where is my welcome?

HAGEN
Hei! Siegfried!
My speedy hero!
Whence did you sweep in?

SIEGFRIED
From Brünnhilde's rock.
'twas there that I drew the breath
with which you were waked.
So fast flew I back here.
Gunther and Brünnhild are slow:
the boat will bear them home.

'I drew the breath with which you
were waked' – a powerful piece
of imagery!

HAGEN
You mastered Brünnhild?

SIEGFRIED
Where is Gutrun?

HAGEN
Hoiho! Gutrune!
Hurry here!
Siegfried is back;
do not delay!

SIEGFRIED
You both shall hear
the tale of Brünnhild's fate.
Now give me greeting,
Gibich's child!
I bring good tidings for us all.

GUTRUNE
Freia grüsse dich
zu aller Frauen Ehre!

SIEGFRIED
Frei und hold
sei nun mir Frohem:
zum Weib gewann ich dich heut.

GUTRUNE
So folgt Brünnhild meinem
    Bruder?

SIEGFRIED
Leicht ward die Frau ihm gefreit.

GUTRUNE
Sengte das Feuer ihn nicht?

Gutrune

SIEGFRIED
Ihn hätt es auch nicht versehrt,
doch ich durchschritt es für *ihn*,
da dich ich wollt erwerben.

GUTRUNE
Und dich hat es verschont?

Loge

SIEGFRIED
Mich freute die schwebende Brunst.

GUTRUNE
Hielt Brünnhild dich für Gunther?

Tarnhelm   *Loge*

SIEGFRIED
Ihm glich ich auf ein *Haar*:
der Tarnhelm wirkte das,
wie Hagen tüchtig es wies.

Loge

HAGEN
Dir gab ich guten Rat.

Loge

GUTRUNE
So zwangst du das kühne Weib?

Tarnhelm

SIEGFRIED
Sie *wich* – *Gun*thers Kraft.

GUTRUNE
Und vermählte sie sich dir?

GUTRUNE
Freia give you joy,
by woman's fairest favour!

SIEGFRIED
Now be kind
and grant me comfort:
today I won you as wife!

GUTRUNE
Does fair Brünnhild follow
  Gunther?

SIEGFRIED
Soon was she wooed as his wife.

GUTRUNE
Was he not foiled by the flames?

SIEGFRIED
He could have conquered the blaze,
but I passed through in his place,
for I so wished to win you.

GUTRUNE
And you kept yourself safe?

SIEGFRIED
I laughed at the flickering flames.

GUTRUNE
To Brünnhild you were Gunther?

SIEGFRIED
We looked so much alike.
The *Tarnhelm* saw to that,
as Hagen truly foretold.

HAGEN
I gave you good advice!

GUTRUNE
You mastered the dauntless maid?

SIEGFRIED
She felt – Gunther's force.

GUTRUNE
Did she give herself to you?

SIEGFRIED

Ihrem Mann gehorchte Brünnhild

Amnesia   eine volle bräutliche *Nacht.*

GUTRUNE

Als ihr Mann doch galtest du?

SIEGFRIED

Bei Gutrune weilte Siegfried.

GUTRUNE

Doch zur Seite war ihm
  Brünnhild?

SIEGFRIED

Nothung *Treaty* *Sword* *Hagen*   Zwischen *Ost* und West der Nord:

Bloodbrothers   so na*h* – *w*ar Brünnhild ihm fern.

GUTRUNE

Wie empfing Gunther sie nun von
  dir?

SIEGFRIED

Durch des Feuers verlöschende
Loge   *Lo*he
im Frühnebel vom Felsen
folgte sie mir zu Tal;
dem Strande nah,
flugs die Stelle
Tarnhelm *Loge*   *tausch*te Gunther mit mir:
durch des Geschmeides Tugend
Horn Call   wünscht ich mich schnell hieher.
Ein starker Wind nun treibt
die Trauten den Rhein herauf:
Gutrune   drum rüstet jetzt den Em*pfang*!

GUTRUNE

Amnesia   Siegfried, mächtigster *Mann*!
Wie fasst mich Furcht vor dir!

HAGEN

In der Ferne seh ich ein Segel.

SIEGFRIED

So sagt dem Boten Dank!

GUTRUNE

Lasset uns sie hold empfangen,

SIEGFRIED
To her husband yielded Brünnhild
in that blissful nuptial night.

GUTRUNE
But her husband – it was you?

SIEGFRIED
With Gutrune was her Siegfried.

GUTRUNE
Yet my Siegfried lay with
  Brünnhild?

SIEGFRIED [pointing to his sword]
Between east and west lies north:
so near – was Brünnhild – so far.

GUTRUNE
How did you place her in Gunther's
  hands?

SIEGFRIED
Through the fast fading flames of
  the fire,
– the mist sank on the mountain –
Brünnhilde followed me.
When near the shore,
all at once
stood Gunther where I had stood.
I, by the Tarnhelm's magic,
wished myself into your arms.
The breezes blow their boat
right merrily up the Rhine.
Make haste to welcome them
  home!

GUTRUNE
Siegfried! Mightiest of men!
I stand in awe of you.

HAGEN
I can see a sail on the river.

SIEGFRIED
Then thank your messenger!

GUTRUNE
Let us give a gracious greeting,

Gutrune cross-examines Siegfried,
skilfully and persistently. He
eventually exonerates himself,
aided by the Sword motif on
trumpet and horns, with the
Treaty motif in the strings con-
firming Siegfried's tale. Unfortu-
nately, a third motif is heard at
the same time, that of Hagen (on
bassoons and double basses).

The flames no longer burn as
Siegfried conducts the conquered
Brünnhilde from her rock down to
the valley. Loge's services are no
longer required here. They will
soon be needed elsewhere for a
weightier purpose.

dass heiter sie und gern hier weile!

Gutrune *Du*, Hagen, minnig
rufe die Mannen
nach Gibichs Hof zur Hochzeit!
Frohe Frauen
ruf ich zum Fest:
Gutrune der Freudigen folgen sie *gern*.
Rastest du, schlimmer Held?

SIEGFRIED
Dir zu helfen, ruh ich aus.

to make her feel at home with
    loved ones.
You, Hagen, sweetly
summon the vassals,
to witness both our weddings.
Merry maids
I'll fetch to the feast.
My happiness shall be their joy.
Will you rest, awesome man?

SIEGFRIED
Helping you is my repose.
[together they go into the hall]

One translator has rendered
'Rastest du, schlimmer Held?' as
'Wilt thou sleep, naughty guest?'

II. Akt: 3. Szene

		HAGEN
Grief		*Hoi*ho! Hoihohoho!
		Ihr Gibichsmannen,
		machet euch auf!
		Wehe! Wehe!
	Gutrune	Waffen! Waffen!
		Waffen durchs Land!
		Gute Waffen!
		Starke Waffen,
Gibichungen	Götterdämmerung	scharf zum *Streit*.
		Not ist da!
	Grief	Not! *We*he! Wehe!
		Hoiho! Hoihohoho!

DIE MANNEN

Was tost das Horn?
Was ruft es zu Heer?
Wir kommen mit Wehr,
wir kommen mit Waffen!

Hagen — Ha*ge*n! Hagen!
Hoiho! Hoiho!
Welche Not ist da?
Welcher Feind ist nah?

Gibichungen — Wer gibt uns *Streit*?
Ist Gunther in Not?
Wir kommen mit Waffen,
mit scharfer Wehr.

Gutrune — Hoiho! Ho! Hagen!

HAGEN
Rüstet euch wohl
und rastet nicht;
Gunther sollt ihr empfahn:
ein Weib hat der gefreit.

DIE MANNEN
Drohet ihm Not?
Drängt ihn der Feind?

Act II: Scene 3

[Hagen mounts a rock and blows a
cow-horn]

HAGEN
Hoiho! Hoihohoho!
You men of Gibich,
answer my call!
Rack and ruin!
Weapons! Weapons!
Arm all the land!
Doughty weapons,
deadly weapons,
firm and fierce!
Foes are near!
Foes! Rack and ruin!
Hoiho! Hoihohoho!

THE VASSALS [rushing in from different
directions, fully armed]
Why blares the horn?
What strident alarms?
We come with our arms!
We come with our weapons!
Hagen! Hagen!
Hoiho! Hoiho!
Say what hazard's here!
Say what foe is near!
Who wages war?
Is Gunther in need?
We come with our weapons,
with mighty arms!
Hoiho! Ho! Hagen!

HAGEN
Arm yourselves well
and waste no time!
Welcome Gunther, your lord:
your lord, and your lord's wife!

THE VASSALS
What is his need?
Where is the foe?

The Götterdämmerung motif on
'Not ist da' ('Foes are near') gives
Hagen's statement a cosmic
dimension.

HAGEN
Ein freisliches Weib
führet er heim.

DIE MANNEN
Ihm folgen der Magen
feindliche Mannen?

HAGEN
Liebe-Tragik   *Ein*sam fährt er:
keiner folgt.

DIE MANNEN
So bestand er die Not?
Horn Call   So bestand er den *Kampf*?
Sag es an!

HAGEN
Der Wurmtöter
Horn Call   wehrte der *Not*:
Siegfried, der Held,
der schuf ihm Heil!

DIE MANNEN
Was soll ihm das Heer nun noch
     helfen?

HAGEN
Starke Stiere
sollt ihr schlachten;
am Weihstein fliesse
Wotan ihr Blut!

DIE MANNEN
Was, Hagen, was heissest du uns
     dann?

HAGEN
Einen Eber fällen
sollt ihr für Froh!
Einen stämmigen Bock
stechen für Donner!
Schafe aber
schlachtet für Fricka,
dass gute Ehe sie gebe!

DIE MANNEN
Schlugen wir Tiere,
was schaffen wir dann?

HAGEN
A warrior wife
Gunther has won.

THE VASSALS
Do furious kinsmen
follow our master?

HAGEN
Safe is he,
assailed by none.

THE VASSALS
Then the peril has passed?
Then the foe has been fought?
Tell us all!

HAGEN
The dragon-slayer
fought for his friend:
Siegfried alone
stood by his side.

THE VASSALS
Then why have you called us to
    battle?

HAGEN
Sturdy steers
must now be slaughtered;
let Wotan's altar
ooze with their blood.

THE VASSALS
Then, Hagen, what would you have
    us do?

HAGEN
Let a boar be butchered:
blood-gift for Froh;
and the doughtiest goat
offered to Donner!
Sheep must then
be slaughtered for Fricka,
that she may smile on the marriage!

THE VASSALS
When we have slain them,
what shall we do next?

HAGEN
Das Trinkhorn nehmt,
von trauten Fraun
mit Met und Wein
wonnig gefüllt!

DIE MANNEN
Das Trinkhorn zur Hand,
wie halten wir es dann?

HAGEN
Rüstig gezecht,
bis der Rausch euch zähmt!
Alles den Göttern zu Ehren,
dass gute Ehe sie geben!

DIE MANNEN

Gross Glück und Heil
lacht nun dem Rhein,
da Hagen, der Grimme,
so lustig mag sein!
Der Hagedorn
sticht nun nicht mehr;
zum Hochzeitrufer
Gutrune ward er be*stellt.*

HAGEN
Nun lasst das Lachen,
mutge Mannen!
Empfangt Gunthers Braut!
Gutrune Brünnhilde naht dort mit *ihm.*
Hold seid der Herrin,
Hagen helfet ihr treu:
traf sie ein Leid,
rasch seid zur Rache!

DIE MANNEN
Gutrune *Heil! Heil!*
Willkommen! Willkommen!
Willkommen, Gunther!
Hagen Heil! Heil!

HAGEN
Your drinking horns!
Let merry maids
pour wine and mead,
brim-full and brave!

THE VASSALS
The horns in our hands,
what next are we to do?

HAGEN
Freely carouse,
till you fall like logs!
All to appease the eternals:
then they will welcome the
    wedlock.

THE VASSALS [bursting into loud
laughter]
Laughter and joy
comes to the Rhine,
when Hagen, grim Hagen
is blithe and benign.
Our *Hagedorn*
harms us no more;
our marriage-herald
drinks with his friends.

HAGEN [now standing among the vassals]
Leave o'er your laughter,
valiant vassals!
Now welcome the bride!
Brünnhild and Gunther are here.
Love your new lady,
pledge her your aid!
Should she be wronged,
rush to avenge her!
[the boat with Gunther and Brünnhilde
appears]

THE VASSALS
Hail! Hail!
Be welcome! Be welcome!
Be welcome, Gunther!
Hail! Hail!
[several men leap into the river to haul the
boat in]

Hagen, the master orator, plays
on the vassals' emotions. He
alarms them, then allays their
fears; he feeds them vital information, he makes their adrenalin
flow until they are putty in his
hands.

'Hagedorn' (hawthorn) is Hagen.

'Rush to avenge her!' Hagen
secures the vassals' watchfulness
so that they may witness
Brünnhilde's impending denunci-
ation of Siegfried and, later, may
condone Hagen's murderous
deed.

ii. Akt: 4. Szene

DIE MANNEN

Gibichungen
Heil dir, Gunther!
Heil dir und deiner Braut!
Willkommen!

Ride

GUNTHER
Brünnhild, die hehrste Frau,
Gibichungen bring ich euch her zum *Rhein*.
Ein edleres Weib
ward nie gewonnen.
Der Gibichungen Geschlecht,
gaben die Götter ihm Gunst,
zum höchsten Ruhm
rag es nun auf!

DIE MANNEN
Gibichungen Heil dir,
glücklicher Gibichung!

Gutrune   *Ride*

GUNTHER
Gutrune Gegrüsst sei, teurer Held;
gegrüsst, holde Schwester!
Hagen *Dich* seh ich froh ihm zur Seite,
Liebe-Tragik der dich zum *Weib* gewann.
Zwei selge Paare
Gutrune seh ich hier prangen:
Brünnhild und Gunther,
Sword *Hagen* Gutrun und *Siegfried*!
Revenge *Crisis*
Revenge *Fate*
Crisis

DIE MANNEN
Fate *Crisis* Was *ist* ihr? Ist sie entrückt?
Tarnhelm *Amnesia*
Hagen SIEGFRIED
Gutrune Was *müht* Brünnhilde's *Blick*?

Act II: Scene 4

[Gunther leads Brünnhilde ceremoniously
ashore. She is pale and averts her eyes.]

THE VASSALS
Welcome, Gunther!
Hail, Gunther and your bride!
Be welcome!

GUNTHER
Brünnhild, the rarest bride,
home to the Rhine I bring.
A nobler wife
was never wedded.
The Gibichungs now are blest,
graced by the gods with their love.
To great renown
shall we be raised.

THE VASSALS
All hail,
glorious Gibichung!
[attended by women, Siegfried and Gutrune
now appear]

GUNTHER
I greet you, honoured friend,
and you, sweetest sister!
Winsomest woman, close by him
who won you for his wife.
Two fair betrothals,
may they both flourish:
Brünnhild and Gunther,
Gutrun and Siegfried!
[Brünnhilde raises her eyes and is startled
to see Siegfried]

SOME VASSALS
What ails her? Why such distress?

SIEGFRIED [calmly]
What irks Brünnhilde's eyes?

Gunther presents Brünnhilde to
his court; his mock-heroic, diatonic bluster hides the hollow-
ness of a weak man's vanity.

BRÜNNHILDE
Siegfried ... hier ...! Gutrune ...?

SIEGFRIED
*Gut*hers milde Schwester:
mir vermählt
wie Gunther du.

Gutrune

BRÜNNHILDE
Ich ... Gunther ...? Du lügst!

Fate

Brünnhilde   *Hagen*   Mir schwindet das Licht ...

Siegfried – kennt mich nicht?

SIEGFRIED
Brünnhilde   Gun*ther*, deinem Weib ist übel!
Erwache, Frau!
Ring   Hier steht dein Gatte.

BRÜNNHILDE

Curse   Ha! – Der Ring
an seiner Hand!
Liebe-Tragik   Er ... Siegfried?

DIE MANNEN
Nibelungen Hate   Was *ist? Was* ist?

HAGEN
Nibelungen Hate⌐   Jetzt merket klug,
was die Frau euch klagt!

BRÜNNHILDE
Nibelungen Hate⌐   Einen Ring sah ich
an deiner Hand.
Nicht dir gehört er,
ihn entriss mir
dieser Mann!
Wie mochtest von ihm
den Ring du empfahn?

SIEGFRIED
Nibelungen Hate⌐   Den Ring empfing ich
Rhinegold   nicht von ihm.
Grief

BRÜNNHILDE
Grief   *Nibelungen Hate*⌐   Nahmst du von mir den *Ring*,

BRÜNNHILDE
Siegfried ... here ...! Gutrune ...?

SIEGFRIED
Gunther's gentle sister.
She is mine,
as you are his.

BRÜNNHILDE
I ... Gunther ...? You lie!
[She appears to faint. Siegfried supports
her.]
The light has gone out.
[she looks Siegfried in the face]
Siegfried – knows me not.

SIEGFRIED
Gunther, see, your wife is ailing!
Awaken, wife!
There stands your husband.

BRÜNNHILDE [sees the ring on Siegfried's
outstretched finger]
Ha! – that ring
upon his hand!
He ... Siegfried?

SOME VASSALS
What's this? What's this?

HAGEN
Now listen well
to this woman's words!

BRÜNNHILDE
On your hand there
I saw a ring.
It is not your ring.
He who stole it –
there he stands! [pointing to Gunther]
How came then the ring
from his hand to yours?

SIEGFRIED [regarding the ring on his finger]
The ring –
I had it not from him.

BRÜNNHILDE [to Gunther]
You robbed me of my ring,

Brünnhilde sees her ring on
Siegfried's finger. It should be on
Gunther's. She concludes, cor-
rectly, that it was Siegfried, not
Gunther, who robbed her of it.
But Siegfried denies this. His
amnesia does not extend back to
the period before he knew
Brünnhilde, when he took the
ring from Fafner's lair.

Nibelungen Hate | *Gold's Dominion*
Gold's Dominion
Amnesia

durch den ich *dir* vermählt,
so melde ihm dein *Recht*,
fordre zu*rück* das Pfand!

GUNTHER

Nibelungen Hate

Den Ring? Ich gab ihm keinen:
Doch – kennst du ihn auch gut?

BRÜNNHILDE

Nibelungen Hate
Amnesia   *Rhinegold*   *Tarnhelm*   *Revenge*
Grief
Ring
Revenge

Wo bärgest du den Ring,
den du von *mir er*beutet?
Ha! – Dieser war es,
der mir den Ring entriss:
Siegfried, der trugvolle Dieb!

SIEGFRIED

Ring

Fafner

Rhinegold
Nibelungen Hate

Von keinem Weib
kam mir der Reif;
noch war's ein Weib,
dem ich ihn abgewann:
genau erkenn ich
des Kampfes *Lohn*,
den vor Neidhöhl einst ich bestand,
als den starken Wurm ich erschlug.

HAGEN

Nibelungen Hate
Rhinegold

Hagen   *Siegfried*

Amnesia
Hagen

Brünnhild, kühne Frau,
kennst du genau den Ring?
Ist's der, den *du* Gunther gabst?
so ist er *sein*,
und Siegfried gewann ihn durch
    Trug,
den der Treulose büssen soll!

BRÜNNHILDE

Hagen   *Ring*

Revenge

Betrug! Betrug!
Schändlichster Betrug!
Verrat! Verrat!
Wie noch nie er gerächt!

GUTRUNE

Revenge

Verrat? An wem?

DIE MANNEN

Verrat? Verrat?

FRAUEN

Verrat? An wem?

when I became your bride.
Now claim it as your own!
Make him return the ring!

GUNTHER [perplexed]
The ring? No ring I gave him.
But is it really yours?

BRÜNNHILDE
Where have you hid the ring
which from my hand you wrested?
Ha! He it was
has robbed me of my ring:
Siegfried, the treacherous thief!

SIEGFRIED
No woman
vouchsafed me this ring,
nor did I wrest it
from a woman's hand.
This ring, I know,
was my rich reward,
for at Neidhöhl fierce was the fight:
fierce the dragon whom I
    destroyed.

Unused to the art of deception,
Siegfried has made a thorough
mess of wooing Brünnhilde. He
forgot to hand the ring to Gunther. But then, the ring had been
cursed by Alberich, and Siegfried's
fatal error is just another mani-
festation of the power of the
curse.

HAGEN [stepping between them]
Brünnhild, valiant wife,
how do you know this ring?
If Gunther had it from you,
then it is his,
but Siegfried has gained it by
    guile,
and the traitor shall make amends.

BRÜNNHILDE [with vehement passion]
Betrayed! Betrayed!
Shamefully betrayed!
Deceived! Deceived!
Deadly be my revenge!

GUTRUNE
Deceived? By whom?

THE VASSALS
Betrayed? Betrayed?

WOMEN
Betrayed? By whom?

BRÜNNHILDE

Walhall — Heilge *Göt*ter,
himmlische Lenker!
Revenge — *Raun*tet ihr dies
Nibelungen Hate — in eurem Rat?
Liebesnot — Lehrt ihr mich *Lei*den,
Nibelungen Hate — wie keiner sie litt?
Grief — Schuft ihr mir *Schmach*,
wie nie sie geschmerzt?
Liebesnot — Ratet nun *Ra*che,
wie nie sie gerast!
Liebesnot — Zündet mir *Zorn*,
wie noch nie er gezähmt!
Heisset Brünnhild,
Grief — ihr Herz zu zerbrechen,
den zu zertrümmern,
der sie betrog!

GUNTHER

Brünnhild, Gemahlin!
Revenge — Mäss'ge dich!

BRÜNNHILDE

Revenge — Weich fern, Verräter!
Selbst Verratner!
Wisset denn alle:
nicht ihm –
dem Manne dort
Revenge — bin ich ver*mählt*.

FRAUEN

Revenge — Siegfried? Gutruns Gemahl?

DIE MANNEN

Gutruns Gemahl?

BRÜNNHILDE

Liebe-Tragik — *Er* zwang mir Lust
Revenge — und Liebe ab.

SIEGFRIED

Achtest du so
der eignen Ehre?
Revenge — Die Zunge, die sie lästert,
muss ich der Lüge sie zeihen?
Hagen — Hört, ob ich Treue brach!
Bloodbrothers — *Blut*brüderschaft
hab ich Gunther ge*schwo*ren:
Nothung — No*thung, das wer*te Schwert,
Sword

BRÜNNHILDE
Holy gods,
you heavenly guardians!
Did you ordain
this dread decree?
Pain you have sent me,
past patience and plaint.
Shame is my share,
degrading and grim.
Now vouch me vengeance,
as never was vowed!
Rouse in me wrath,
such as none can arrest!
Then, though Brünnhilde's
heart has been broken,
let the foul traitor
die a foul death!

GUNTHER
Brünnhild, dear consort,
calm yourself!

BRÜNNHILDE
Away, deceiver
and deceived one!
Listen, you people:
not he,
but that man there –
he is my lord!

WOMEN
Siegfried? Gutrune's spouse?

VASSALS
Gutrune's spouse?

BRÜNNHILDE
He had his
ardent way with me.

SIEGFRIED
Have you no care
for your own honour?
Your tongue is swift to slander,
but your own tongue is a traitor.
Hear, how I kept my faith!
Bloodbrotherhood
have I sworn unto Gunther.
Nothung, my gallant sword,

Can Brünnhilde's raging lust for vengeance be explained? In *The Winter's Tale* Polixines says of Leontes:
> 'This jealousy
> is for a precious creature;
> as she's rare,
> must it be great.'

Siegfried remembers selectively. He has forgotten (Freud would have said repressed) his physical attack on Brünnhilde. In fact, he is too ashamed to remember.

Treaty + Hagen wahrte der Treue *Eid*;
Sword⌉ mich trennte seine Schärfe
  Revenge von diesem traur'gen Weib.

BRÜNNHILDE
Revenge⌉ Du listiger Held,
  sieh, wie du lügst!
  Wie auf dein Schwert
  du schlecht dich berufst!
Sword Wohl kenn ich sei*ne* Schärfe,
Consorts doch kenn ich auch die *Schei*de,
  darin so wonnig
Sword ruh' an *der* Wand
Nothung *Consorts* *No*thung, der treu*e* Freund,
  als die Traute sein Herr sich gefreit.

DIE MANNEN
  Wie? Brach er die Treue?
Consorts Trübte er Gunthers Ehre?

FRAUEN
Consorts Brach er die Treue?
Nibelungen Hate⌉

Grief + Nibelungen Hate⌉ *Consorts* GUNTHER
  Geschändet wär ich,
  schmählich bewahrt,
Nibelungen Hate gäbst du die Rede
Consorts *Grief* nicht ihr zu*rück*!

GUTRUNE
Grief⌉ Treulos, Siegfried,
  sännest du Trug?
Loge + Consorts Be*zeu*ge, dass jene
  falsch dich zeiht!

DIE MANNEN
Loge + Consorts⌉ Reinige dich,
  bist du im Recht!
  Schweige die Klage!
  Grief Schwöre den Eid!

SIEGFRIED
  Schweig ich die Klage,
  schwör ich den Eid:
  wer von euch wagt
Hagen *Revenge* seine Waffe da*ran*?

guarded the sacred oath.
Its sharp edge was the barrier
against this ill-starred bride.

BRÜNNHILDE
You lord of deceit,
look how you lie!
Shaming your sword
to swear to your crime!
Well do I know its sharp edge,
I also know the scabbard,
wherein so snugly
slept by the wall
Nothung, the faithful friend,
when its master would sleep by my
    side.

THE VASSALS [indignantly]
What? Siegfried a traitor?
Injured is Gunther's honour?

WOMEN
Siegfried a traitor?

GUNTHER [to Siegfried]
Dishonoured were I,
slurred were my name:
this woman's slander
you must confound.

GUTRUNE
Faithless, Siegfried?
False to us all?
Bear witness that worthless
are her words!

THE VASSALS
Answer her taunts,
if you are true!
Silence her slander!
Swear us an oath!

SIEGFRIED
Yes, I will answer!
Yes, I am true!
Whose is the weapon
shall challenge my words?

Brünnhilde is referring to all those
nights when Siegfried was still
her beloved champion. Siegfried
does not remember them, but
speaks of that one night when
Nothung ensured their sexual
abstinence.

HAGEN

Hagen	*Revenge*	Meines Speeres Spitze
		wag ich daran:
Crisis	*Atonement*	sie *wahr* in Ehren den Eid.
	Revenge	

SIEGFRIED

		Helle Wehr!
	Hagen	Heilige *Waf*fe!
	Revenge	Hilf meinem ewigen *Ei*de!
		Bei des Speeres Spitze
	Hagen	sprech ich den *Eid*:
	Revenge	Spitze, achte des *Spruchs*!
	Murder	Wo *Schar*fes mich schneidet,
	Revenge	schneide du *mich*;
	Murder	wo der *Tod* mich soll treffen,
	Revenge	treffe du *mich*:
		klagte das Weib dort wahr,
Valkyrie Cry	*Ride*	brach ich dem Bruder die Treu!

BRÜNNHILDE

		Helle Wehr!
Hagen		Heilige *Waf*fe!
	Revenge	*Hilf* meinem ewigen Eide!
		Bei des Speeres *Spitz*e
		sprech ich den Eid:
Hagen	*Revenge*	*Spitz*e, achte des Spruchs!
	Murder	Ich *wei*he deine Wucht,
Nothung *Hagen*	*Revenge*	dass sie ihn werfe!
	Murder	Deine *Schär*fe segne ich,
Nothung *Hagen*	*Revenge*	dass sie ihn schneide:
		denn, brach seine Eide er all,
		schwur Meineid jetzt dieser Mann!

DIE MANNEN

	Hilf, Donner,
	tose dein Wetter,
Consorts	zu schweigen die *wü*tende
	Schmach!

SIEGFRIED

	Gunther, wehr deinem *Weib*e,
Consorts	das schamlos Schande dir lügt!
Liebesnot	Gönnt ihr Weil und Ruh,
	der wilden Felsenfrau,

HAGEN
Then let Hagen's spear-point
challenge your words:
it guards the honour of oaths.
[The vassals form a circle round Siegfried
and Hagen. Hagen holds out his spear
and Siegfried lays two fingers on the spear-
point.]

The spear oath is an early form of
lie-detector: if your hand
trembles, the spear-point draws
blood.

SIEGFRIED
Shining steel!
Holiest weapon!
Come to the aid of my honour!
On this piercing spear-point
swear I this oath;:
spear-point, witness my words!
If steel ever strikes me,
yours be the stroke;
and if death overpowers me,
yours be the power:
if what she tells is true,
if I am false to my friend!

Hagen is the manipulator who
has stage managed the whole
oath scene. The falling fifth of his
motif is everywhere.

BRÜNNHILDE [tearing Siegfried's hand
away from the spear and seizing its point]
Shining steel!
Holiest weapon!
Come to the aid of my honour!
On this piercing spear-point
swear I this oath:
spear-point, witness my words!
I consecrate this steel,
that it may strike him;
and I consecrate its point,
that it may pierce him:
for false he has been to his vows,
and false is all he has sworn!

THE VASSALS
Help, Donner!
Send down your thunder,
to silence this grievous disgrace!

The vassals have reached their
verdict: Siegfried is guilty. They
now invoke Donner to create
another storm, to expurgate
Brünnhilde and Gunther's shame.

SIEGFRIED
Gunther, look to your lady,
who dares to damage your name.
Let her rest awhile,
this wrathful mountain maid,

(Consorts)	dass ihre freche Wut sich lege,
	die eines Unholds
	arge List
	wider uns alle erregt!
	Ihr Mannen, kehret euch ab!
	Lasst das Weibergekeif!
	Als Zage weichen wir gern,
Hagen + Loge + Tarnhelm	gilt es mit Zungen den *Streit*.
	Glaub, mehr zürnt es mich als
Tarnhelm	dich,
	dass schlecht ich sie getäuscht:
	der Tarnhelm, dünkt mich fast,
	hat halb mich nur gehehlt.
	Doch Frauengroll
Liebe-Tragik	*frie*det sich bald:
Grief *Consorts*	dass ich *dir* es gewann,
	dankt dir gewiss noch das Weib.
	Munter, ihr Mannen!
Gutrune	Folgt mir zum *Mahl*!
	Froh zur Hochzeit
	helfet, ihr Frauen!
	Wonnige Lust
	lache nun auf!
	In Hof und Hain,
	heiter vor allen
	sollt ihr heute mich sehn.
Liebe-Tragik	*Wen* die Minne freut,
	meinem frohen Mute
Gutrune	tu es der Glückliche *gleich*!

until her shrewish rage is over.
Some evil demon's
evil deed
makes her find fault with us all.
You vassals, be on your way!
Shun the bickering wife!
Like cowards, let us retreat:
this is a battle of tongues.
[to Gunther]
Greater is my grief than
   yours,
that our plot went wrong.
The Tarnhelm, I suspect,
was not a good disguise.
But women's wrath
does not abide.
I have won her for you –
one day she'll thank you for that.
Follow me, fellows!
Come to the feast!
Joyful women,
wait on our wedding!
Show your delight,
laugh now aloud!
In house and field,
joyful and jaunty
shall you find me today.
You who live for love,
let my own good fortune
move you to join in my joy!
[In exuberant mood, Siegfried takes Gutrune
by the arm and leads her away, followed by
the vassals and women. Brünnhilde, Gunther and Hagen are alone. Brünnhilde gazes
sadly and thoughtfully after Siegfried.]

II. Akt: 5. Szene

	Revenge	**BRÜNNHILDE**
Nibelungen Hate	*Murder*	*Wel*ches Unholds List
	Revenge	liegt hier ver*hohl*en?
	Fate	*Wel*ches Zaubers Rat
		*reg*te dies auf?

Wo ist nun mein Wissen
gegen dies Wirrsal?
Wo sind meine Runen
gegen dies Rätsel?

Grief

Ach *Jam*mer, Jammer!

Bequest

Weh, ach Wehe!
All mein Wissen

Consorts

wies ich ihm *zu*!
In seiner Macht
hält er die Magd;
in seinen Banden
fasst er die Beute,
die, jammernd ob ihrer Schmach,

Murder   *Revenge*

jauchzend der Reiche verschenkt!
Wer bietet mir nun das Schwert,
mit dem ich die Bande zerschnitt'?

HAGEN

Hagen

*Ver*traue mir,
betrogne Frau!
Wer dich verriet,
das räche ich.

BRÜNNHILDE
An wem?

HAGEN
An Siegfried, der dich betrog.

BRÜNNHILDE
An Siegfried? ... du?

Liebesglück + Nibelungen Hate

Ein einzger Blick

Amnesia

seines blitzenden *A*uges,

Gloom and discontent saturate
the brief orchestral introduction.
The mere names of the leitmotifs
give warning of the horror of the
ensuing scene.

Act II: Scene 5

BRÜNNHILDE [brooding]
Dreadful demon's craft!
Monstrous its magic!
Spiteful wizard's spell!
Chaos is here!
What help is my wisdom
in this bewitchment?
What help are my runes
against such riddle!
Alas, what sorrow!
Tears and anguish!
All my wisdom
won he from me.
My master he –
I am his maid.
Confined in bondage,
I am his booty:
the pitiful, lowly prize
Siegfried has given away.
Who offers me now a sword,
the sword that will sever these
    bonds?

At 'Who offers me now a sword?'
Wagner commented: 'That is
dreadful, dreadful, dreadful.'
[Heinrich Porges, *Bayreuther
Blätter*, 1896]

HAGEN [whispers to her]
Leave that to me,
outwitted wife!
Shameful offence
shall be avenged.

BRÜNNHILDE
On whom?

HAGEN
On Siegfried! For his deceit!

BRÜNNHILDE
On Siegfried? ... you? [with a
bitter smile]
One single flash
from the eyes of the traitor,

Schopenhauer maintained that a
person's eyes would always
express the true personality,
whatever the disguise.

		das selbst durch die Lügen-
		gestalt
	Liebesglück	*leucht*end strahlte zu mir,
	Horn Call	deinen *be*sten Mut
		machte er bangen!

HAGEN
Doch meinem Speere
spart' ihn sein Meineid?

BRÜNNHILDE
Eid und Meineid,

Siegfried — mü*ssige* Acht!

Nibelungen Hate — Nach *Stärk*rem späh,
deinen Speer zu waffnen,

Murder — willst du den Stärksten bestehn!

HAGEN
Wohl kenn ich Siegfrieds
siegende Kraft,

Loge — wie schwer im Kampf er zu *fäll*en;
drum raune nun du
mir klugen Rat,
wie doch der Recke mir wich'?

BRÜNNHILDE
O Undank, schändlichster Lohn!
Nicht eine Kunst
war mir bekannt,

Siegfried   *Jubilation* — die *zum* Heil nicht half seinem
    Leib!
Unwissend zähmt ihn
mein Zauberspiel,

Revenge   *Nibelungen Hate* — das ihn vor Wunden nun ge*wahrt*.

HAGEN

Murder   *Nibelungen Hate* — So kann keine Wehr ihm schaden?

BRÜNNHILDE

Nibelungen Hate — Im Kampfe nicht;
doch träfst du im Rücken ihn ...

Bequest   *Siegfried* — *Nie*mals, das wusst ich,
wich' er dem Feind,

Sword — nie reicht er fliehend ihm *den*
    *Rück*en:
an ihm drum spart ich den Segen.

which Tarnhelm's disguise could
    not hide,
as it kindled my heart,
and your manliness
turns into terror.

HAGEN
Then shall my spear-point
suffer his falsehood?

BRÜNNHILDE
Faith or falsehood –
meaningless words!
Seek stronger spells
to sustain your weapon,
if you would fight with the best!

HAGEN
Well known is Siegfried's
sovereign might,
well known his prowess in battle.
Then whisper to me
some secret spell,
to hasten him to his doom.

BRÜNNHILDE
Rejected! Wretched reward!
There is no web
that I can weave
and that would not lengthen his
    life.
He does not know
of my guardian spells
that grant him safety from all harm.

As a former Valkyrie, Brünnhilde
is familiar with human bravery,
pride and frailty, but she is incap-
able of fathoming wickedness.
She is easy prey for Hagen.

HAGEN
Then no weapon's point can
    wound him?

BRÜNNHILDE
In battle, none; yet,
if you could strike his back ...
never, but never
would he give way,
nor would he turn his back in
    battle:
and there my spells do not guard
    him.

The *Volsunga Saga* tells of a leaf
from a linden tree which fell
between Siegfried's shoulders as
he covered himself with the hard-
ening dragon-blood. In the
Thidrek Saga Siegfried could not
reach between his shoulder
blades, thus leaving a vulnerable
spot. Wagner eschewed such acci-
dental motivations: 'Never ...
would he turn his back in battle,
and there my spells do not guard
him.'

HAGEN

Revenge Und dort trifft ihn mein *Speer*!

Auf, Gunther,
Atonement edler Gibichung!
Hier steht dein starkes Weib;
was hängst du dort im Harm?

GUNTHER

Atonement O Schmach!
O Schande!
Wehe mir,
Liebe-Tragik   *Revenge* dem *jam*mervollsten Man*ne*!

HAGEN

In Schande liegst du;
leugn ich das?

BRÜNNHILDE

O feiger Mann!
Nibelungen Hate Falscher Ge*noss*!
Hinter dem Helden
hehltest du dich,
dass Preise des Ruhmes
er dir erränge!
Tief wohl sank das teure
Geschlecht,
Revenge das solche Zagen gezeugt!

GUNTHER

Revenge Betrüger ich – und betrogen!
Verräter ich – und verraten!
Zermalmt mir das Mark!
Zerbrecht mir die Brust!
Hagen Hilf, *Ha*gen!
Hilf meiner Ehre!
Liebe-Tragik *Hilf* deiner Mutter,
Revenge die dich – auch ja gebar!

HAGEN

Revenge *Dir* hilft kein Hirn,
dir hilft keine Hand:
Grief dir hilft nur – Siegfrieds Tod!

GUNTHER

Hagen   *Revenge*   *Grief* *Sieg*frieds Tod?

HAGEN

Grief   *Bloodbrothers* Nur der sühnt deine Schmach!

HAGEN
And there settles my spear!
[he immediately turns to Gunther]
Up, Gunther,
noble Gibichung!
Here stands your warlike wife:
why hang your head in grief?

GUNTHER
O shame!
Dishonoured!
Woe is me:
no man has known such torment!

HAGEN
In shame you stand,
in shame indeed.

BRÜNNHILDE [to Gunther]
You timid man,
treacherous spouse!
Hiding behind him
like a sneak thief:
your richest reward –
procured by a traitor!
Rotten is the wondrous
  race
that breeds such weaklings as you.

GUNTHER
Deceived am I, the deceiver!
Betrayed am I, the betrayer!
It cuts to the core,
it harrows my heart.
Help, Hagen,
stand by my honour!
Stand by your mother,
for you, too, are her son!

HAGEN
Not head nor hand
can help you now:
no help but – Siegfried's death!

GUNTHER [horrified]
Siegfried's death!

HAGEN
His death for your disgrace!

GUNTHER

Bloodbrothers Blutbrüderschaft
schwuren wir uns!

HAGEN

Des Bundes Bruch
Atonement sühne nun Blut!

GUNTHER

Atonement Brach er den Bund?

HAGEN

Atonement Da er dich verriet!

GUNTHER

Verriet er mich?

BRÜNNHILDE

Dich verriet er,
und mich verrietet ihr alle!
Wär ich gerecht,
alles Blut der Welt
Revenge büsste mir nicht eure Schuld!
Murder *Brünnhilde* Doch des *einen* Tod
taugt mir für alle:
Murder *Sieg*fried falle!
Hagen *Nibelungen Hate* zur Sühne für sich und *euch*!

HAGEN

Er falle – dir zum Heil!
Ungeheure Macht wird dir,
gewinnst von ihm du den Ring,
den der Tod ihm wohl nur
entreisst.

GUNTHER

Consorts *Brünn*hildes Ring?

HAGEN

Grief *Gold's Dominion* Des *Ni*belungen *Reif.*

GUNTHER

Revenge So wär es Siegfrieds *En*de!

HAGEN

Grief *Revenge* *Uns* allen frommt sein Tod.

GUNTHER

Gutrune Doch *Gu*trune, ach,

GUNTHER
Bloodbrotherhood
fused us as friends!

HAGEN
His broken oath
calls for his blood!

GUNTHER
His broken oath?

HAGEN
He betrayed his friend!

GUNTHER
Am I betrayed?

BRÜNNHILDE
He betrayed you!
To me you all have been traitors!
Blood be for blood,
yet a world of blood
could not atone for your crimes!
Let the death of *one*
serve as a token:
Siegfried be broken!
He pays for the sins of all!

HAGEN [whispers to Gunther]
So be it – to save *you*!
All the world is yours to rule,
for you will gather the ring
which his death alone can bestow.

GUNTHER
Brünnhilde's ring?

HAGEN
The Nibelung's own ring!

GUNTHER [sighing]
Is this the end of Siegfried?

HAGEN
His death shall serve us all.

GUNTHER
But Gutrune, ah!

This scene fulfils the prophecy of the 'Song of the Sybil' in the Edda:
> 'Brother shall smite brother,
> evil be on earth,
> an age of debauchery,
> a wind-age, a wolf-age:
> no mercy shall be on earth.'

Brünnhilde echoes her father's equally fatal misjudgement when she pronounces: 'Siegfried falle!' In the second act of *Walküre* Wotan had condemned his son to death with the words 'Siegmund falle!'.

(Gutrune) der ich ihn gönnte!
Straften den Gatten wir so,
wie bestünden wir vor ihr?

BRÜNNHILDE
Gutrune Was riet mir mein Wissen?
Was wiesen mich Runen?
Im hilflosen Elend
achtet mir's hell:
Gutrune heisst der Zauber,
der den Gatten mir entzückt!
Hagen *Angst* treffe sie!

HAGEN
Muss sein Tod sie betrüben,
Horn Call verhehlt sei ihr die *Tat*,
Auf muntres Jagen
ziehen wir morgen:
der Edle braust uns voran,
Revenge ein *E*ber bracht ihn da um.

GUNTHER und BRÜNNHILDE
Revenge So soll es sein!
Hagen Siegfried *fal*le!
Revenge *Atonement* *Nibelungen Hate* *Sühn* er *die Schmach*,
die er mir schuf!
Des Eides Treue
hat er getrogen:
mit seinem Blut
büss er die Schuld!
Atonement *All*rauner,
rächender Gott!
Schwurwissender
Eideshort!
Wotan!
Wende dich her!
Weise die schrecklich
Walhall *hei*lige Schar,
hieher zu horchen
Gutrune dem *R*acheschwur!

HAGEN
Nibelungen Hate Sterb er dahin,
der strahlende Held!
Mein ist der Hort,
mir muss er gehören.
Drum sei der Reif
Atonement ihm ent*r*issen.
Alben-Vater,

He is her husband!
Siegfried's blood on our hands,
can we ever face her again?

BRÜNNHILDE [enraged]
My portents predicted,
my runes gave me warning,
what direst distress
now clearly reveals:
Gutrune is the magic
that has robbed me of my lord.
Let her be cursed!

HAGEN [to Gunther]
Since his death must dismay her,
we should conceal the deed.
When we go hunting
early tomorrow,
the hero rushes ahead:
we find him – bled by a boar!

GUNTHER and BRÜNNHILDE
So shall it be!
Siegfried perish!
Purged be my shame
which is his share!
The bonds of friendship
all has he broken:
now let his blood
blot out his guilt!
All-guiding
god of revenge,
oath-witnessing
ward of vows,
Wotan!
Look upon me!
Call up your dreaded
heavenly host,
bid them give ear
to my oath of revenge!

HAGEN
So let him die,
the mettlesome man!
Mine is the hoard,
and I shall command it.
Mine is the ring,
mine for ever.
Niblung father,

				(Atonement)	gefallner Fürst!
					Nachthüter!
					Niblungenherr!
					Alberich!
					Achte auf mich!
					Weise von neuem
		Walhall	Hagen		der *Nib*lungen *Schar*,
					dir zu gehorchen,
			Gutrune		des *Ringes* Herrn!

Gutrune	Hagen	Grief	Revenge
	Grief	Gutrune	Hagen
		Grief + Revenge	Grief

you fallen prince!
Night guardian,
Nibelung lord,
Alberich!
Look upon me!
Bid once again
all the Nibelung host
to bow before you,
the ring's true lord!
[As Gunther and Brünnhilde leave the hall
they meet Siegfried and Gutrune's bridal
procession. At Gutrune's friendly smile,
Brünnhilde turns away in horror. Hagen
urges her to Gunther's side. The curtain
falls.]

Treaties are no longer sacred.
Wotan, whose spear has been
shattered, is awaiting the final
conflagration. So is Loge.
Siegfried has abandoned
Brünnhilde in favour of Gunther
and Gutrune. Brünnhilde instructs
Hagen how to murder Siegfried.
The world has moved into an era
of betrayal and false relations.

Siegfried's funeral; illustration by
Knut Ekwall (1876)

III
Act

Synopsis
Leitmotifs
Libretto

Act III: Story

Wooded Valley on the Rhine

The Rhinemaidens ask Siegfried to return the ring to them: 'A golden ring gleams on your finger. We want it!'

Scene 1
The Rhinemaidens still hope to regain their stolen gold. They hear Siegfried's hunting horn. The hero has become separated from the hunting party, and the Rhinemaidens promise him

rich booty in return for the ring on his finger. Siegfried refuses to part with Brünnhilde's love token, whereupon the Rhinemaidens tell him that he will soon meet his death unless he gives them the doom-laden ring. Siegfried contemplates parting with the ring, but will not surrender it under duress.

Scene 2

Siegfried hears the Gibichung hunting call. Meeting up with the party, he is invited by Hagen to tell them about his ability to understand the language of the birds. This prompts Siegfried to entertain Gunther, Hagen and the assembled huntsmen with the story of his slaying of the dragon and of Mime's death. Skilfully guided by Hagen, Siegfried continues the tale. Aided by Hagen's potion (the antidote to Gutrune's potion of forgetfulness), he now remembers and relates his first sight of Brünnhilde and their rapturous union. Hagen murders him by thrusting his spear into Siegfried's unprotected back. Siegfried invokes his beloved Brünnhilde, then falls back and dies. His body is borne to the Gibichung hall.

Scene 3

Gutrune, seeing Siegfried dead, collapses by his bier. Hagen kills Gunther in the struggle over the dead man's ring. Brünnhilde, now grown wise through her suffering, and understanding Siegfried's unwitting treachery, takes the ring from Siegfried's hand. She has the hero's body placed on a funeral pyre and throws a fiery brand at the logs. She mounts her horse and rides into the flames. The Rhinemaidens retrieve the ring, and as Hagen makes a desperate attempt to gain it for himself they draw him into the depths of the river. Walhall is destroyed by the flames. The end of the gods has come, and the waters of the Rhine engulf the world, which is purified and redeemed from the curse on love. The Assurance motif suggests the possibility of a new beginning.

Act III: Action

1. Orchestra: Prelude
2. The Rhinemaidens
3. Siegfried refuses to surrender the ring
4. Siegfried meets the hunters
5. Siegfried's story
6. Hagen kills Siegfried
7. Orchestra: Funeral Music
8. Gutrune alone
9. Siegfried's body arrives in the hall
10. Hagen kills Gunther
11. Brünnhilde's oration
12. Immolation
13. Orchestra: Götterdämmerung

Brünnhilde rides into the
funeral pyre; illustration by
Arthur Rackham (1911)

III. Akt: 1. Szene

DIE DREI RHEINTÖCHTER
Frau Sonne
sendet lichte Strahlen;
Rhinegold   Nacht liegt in der *Tie*fe:
einst war sie hell,
da heil und hehr
Rhinegold   des Vaters Gold *noch* in ihr
    glänzte.
Rheingold,
klares Gold!
Wie hell du einstens strahltest,
hehrer Stern der Tiefe!
Weiala leia,
wallala leialala.
Frau Sonne,
sende uns den Helden,
Rhinegold   der das Gold uns wieder*gäbe*!
Liess er es uns,
dein lichtes Auge
Rhinegold   neideten *dann wir* nicht länger.
Rheingold,
klares Gold!
Wie froh du dann strahltest,
freier Stern der Tiefe!

WOGLINDE
Ich höre sein Horn.

WELLGUNDE
Der Helde naht.

FLOSSHILDE
Lasst uns beraten!

Act III: Scene 1

The hunt which Hagen mentioned at the end of the previous act is now on. Horns are heard on and off stage. Genesis, Joy and Rhinegold, motifs associated with the Rhinemaidens, lodge the coming scene by the river bank.

[A wooded valley on the Rhine. The three Rhinemaidens, Woglinde, Wellgunde and Flosshilde, swim around in a circle.]

THE THREE RHINEMAIDENS
Fair sunlight
sends us rays of radiance.
Night reigns in the waters.
Once there was light,
when bright and brave
our father's gold would shine upon
    us.
Rhinegold,
gleaming gold!
How goodly was your glow,
o royal star of the river!
Weialala leia,
wallala leialala.
Fair sunlight,
send us soon the hero
who restores our golden treasure.
O bring it back!
Your radiant eye
no more would arouse our envy.
Rhinegold,
gleaming gold!
How great then your glory,
reborn star of the river!
[Siegfried's horn is heard]

The single harp that first accompanies the Rhinemaidens is joined by four off-stage harps for their gurgling 'Weialala leia'. This serves to heighten the tension, just before Siegfried's appearance.

WOGLINDE
I hear Siegfried's horn!

WELLGUNDE
The hero comes.

FLOSSHILDE
Let us take counsel!
[They dive down. Siegfried appears, armed.]

SIEGFRIED
Ein Albe führte mich irr,
dass ich die Fährte verlor.
He, Schelm,
in welchem Berge
bargst du schnell mir das Wild?

DIE DREI RHEINTÖCHTER

Siegfried!

FLOSSHILDE
Was schiltst du so in den Grund?

WELLGUNDE
Welchem Alben bist du gram?

WOGLINDE
Hat dich ein Nicker geneckt?

ALLE DREI
Sag es, Siegfried, sag es uns!

SIEGFRIED
Entzücktet ihr zu euch
den zottigen Gesellen,
der mir verschwand?
Ist's euer Friedel,
euch lustigen Frauen
lass ich ihn gern.

WOGLINDE
Siegfried, was gibst du uns,
wenn wir das Wild dir gönnen?

Rhinegold   *Ring*   **SIEGFRIED**
Noch bin ich beutelos;
so bittet, was ihr begehrt.

Ring⌐   **WELLGUNDE**
Ein goldner Ring
glänzt dir am Finger!

Liebe-Tragik   *Ring*   **ALLE DREI**
Den *gib* uns!

Dragon⌐   **SIEGFRIED**
Einen *Riese*nwurm

SIEGFRIED
Some sprite has led me astray:
I wonder where I can be?
Speak, rogue!
Which mountain cave
conceals now the trail of my prey?

THE THREE RHINEMAIDENS [rising
again and swimming in a circle]
Siegfried!

FLOSSHILDE
What is it angers you so?

WELLGUNDE
Has an elf bedevilled you?

WOGLINDE
Are you annoyed by a gnome?

THE THREE
Tell us, Siegfried, tell us all!

SIEGFRIED
You lured him to your lair,
that shaggy, shambling fellow
whom I have lost?
Is he your lover?
You merry-eyed maids,
I leave him to you.
[the maidens laugh loudly]

WOGLINDE
Siegfried, what will you give,
if we bestow some booty?

SIEGFRIED
Look at my empty hands!
What is it that you desire?

WELLGUNDE
A golden ring
gleams on your finger.

THE THREE
We want it!

SIEGFRIED
With a dragon fiend

(Dragon) erschlug ich um den Reif:
für eines schlechten Bären Tatzen
böt ich ihn nun zum Tausch?

WOGLINDE
Bist du so karg?

WELLGUNDE
So geizig beim Kauf?

FLOSSHILDE
Freigebig
solltest Frauen du sein.

SIEGFRIED
Verzehrt ich an euch mein Gut,
des zürnte mir wohl mein Weib.

FLOSSHILDE
Sie ist wohl schlimm?

WELLGUNDE
Sie schlägt dich wohl?

WOGLINDE
Ihre Hand fühlt schon der Held!

SIEGFRIED
Nun lacht nur lustig zu!
In Harm lass ich euch doch:
denn giert ihr nach dem Ring,
euch Nickern geb ich ihn nie!

FLOSSHILDE
So schön!

WELLGUNDE
So stark!

WOGLINDE
So gehrenswert!

ALLE DREI
Wie schade, dass er geizig ist!

SIEGFRIED
Wie leid ich doch

I fought to win that ring.
Shall paltry paws of humble bears
be bartered for such a ring?

WOGLINDE
O you are mean!

WELLGUNDE
And miserly too!

FLOSSHILDE
Freely spend,
would you win a fair maid!

SIEGFRIED
For wasting my wealth on you,
I fear that my wife would chide.

FLOSSHILDE
Is she so strict?

WELLGUNDE
She thrashes you?

The Rhinemaidens reply with their
own biting repartee.

WOGLINDE
Has he felt Gutrune's fist?
[they burst out laughing]

SIEGFRIED
Well, laugh and have your way!
Your pranks profit you not:
you crave my golden ring,
but never shall it be yours.

FLOSSHILDE
So fair!

WELLGUNDE
So strong!

WOGLINDE
So lovable!

THE THREE
Alas, he is so mean to us!
[they laugh and dive down]

SIEGFRIED
Must I permit

das karge Lob?
Lass ich so mich schmähn?
Kämen sie wieder
zum Wasserrand,
den Ring könnten sie haben.
He! he, ihr muntren
Wasserminnen!
Kommt rasch! Ich schenk euch den
Ring!

Rhinegold

ALLE DREI
Behalt ihn, Held,
und wahr ihn wohl,

Ring
bis du das *Un*heil errätst –

Ring
WOGLINDE und WELLGUNDE
das in dem Ring du hegst.

Ring

ALLE DREI
Froh fühlst du dich dann,

Liebe-Tragik
be*frein* wir dich von dem Fluch.

Ring

SIEGFRIED

Liebe-Tragik
So singet, was ihr wisst!

ALLE DREI
Grief
*Sieg*fried! Siegfried! Siegfried!

Ring
Schlimmes wissen wir *dir.*

Ring
WELLGUNDE
Zu deinem Unheil
wahrst du den Ring!

Ring   *Rhinegold*
ALLE DREI
Aus des *Rheines* Gold
ist der Reif geglüht.

Ring
WELLGUNDE
Der ihn listig geschmiedet –

WOGLINDE
– und schmählich verlor –

Ring
WOGLINDE und WELLGUNDE
– der verfluchte ihn, –

their mocking praise?
Shall I bear this blame?
If they came back
to the river bank,
the ring might I surrender.
Hey! Hey! you merry
water maidens!
Arise! I'll give you my ring!
[he draws the ring from his finger, and the
Rhinemaidens surface again, but now they
are grave and solemn]

THE THREE
Retain the ring
and ward it well,
until you know the ill fate –

WOGLINDE and WELLGUNDE
– that lives within your ring.

THE THREE
Then you might be glad,
were we to counter its curse.

SIEGFRIED [replacing the ring on his
finger]
Then tell me what you know.

THE THREE
Siegfried! Siegfried! Siegfried!
Woe is waiting for you.

WELLGUNDE
Let go the ring
or you will be doomed.

THE THREE
From the Rhine's own gold
the ring was forged.

WELLGUNDE
He who shaped it with slyness –

WOGLINDE
– and lost it with shame –

WOGLINDE and WELLGUNDE
– laid a curse on it, –

As Siegfried changes his mind,
the Rhinemaidens do likewise.

	Curse	**ALLE DREI** – *in* fernster Zeit zu zeugen den Tod
	Ring + Dragon	dem, der ihn *trüg'*.

FLOSSHILDE
Wie den Wurm du fälltest –

WELLGUNDE und **FLOSSHILDE**
– so fällst auch du –

| | *Joy + Forge* | **ALLE DREI**
Und heute noch;
so heissen wir's dir,
*tau*schest den Ring du uns nicht. |

WELLGUNDE und **FLOSSHILDE**
– im tiefen Rhein
ihn zu bergen.

| *Götterdämmerung* | *Genesis*
Fate | **ALLE DREI**
Nur seine Flut
sühnet den Fluch! |

SIEGFRIED
Ihr listigen Frauen,
lasst das sein!
Traut ich kaum eurem Schmeicheln,
euer Drohen schreckt mich noch
  minder!

| *Götterdämmerung*
Ring | *Grief*
Ring
Treaty | **ALLE DREI**
*Sieg*fried! Siegfried!
Wir weisen dich wahr.
*Wei*che, weiche dem *Fluch*!
Ihn flochten nächtlich
webende Nornen
in des Urgesetzes Seil! |

| | *Ring*
Ring
Siegfried | **SIEGFRIED**
Mein Schwert zerschwang einen
  Speer:
des Urgesetzes
ewiges *Seil*,
flochten sie wilde
Flüche hinein, |
| *Nothung* Sword | *Fafner*
Fafner | *Nothung* zerhaut es den Nornen!
Wohl warnte mich einst
vor dem Fluch ein Wurm, |

ALL THREE
– for evermore
to doom to his death
each of its lords.

FLOSSHILDE
As you slew the dragon –

WELLGUNDE and FLOSSHILDE
– shall you be slain –

ALL THREE
– and here, today!
Your fate is foretold,
if you refuse us the ring, –

WELLGUNDE and FLOSSHILDE
– that in the Rhine
we may hide it.

ALL THREE
The Rhine alone
cancels the curse!

SIEGFRIED
You slippery women,
hold your peace!
Fawning never could fool me,
and your threats deserve my
   defiance.

ALL THREE
Siegfried! Siegfried!
We counsel you well.
Flee, o flee from the curse!
At dead of night
by Norns was it woven
in the rope of doom's decree.

SIEGFRIED
My sword once shattered a
   spear:
the timeless rope
of doom's decree,
even though curses
cling to its cords,
Nothung shall slash it asunder!
A dragon forewarned me
to flee the curse,

In the *Thidrek Saga* two nixies in the Danube predict Hagen's (!) death, whereupon he kills them both.

The Rhinemaidens reveal their sombre aspect as they predict Siegfried's death. Their new function resembles that of Brünnhilde, when she informed Siegmund of his impending demise (in *Walküre*, Act II).

Liebe-Tragik   *Joy*   *Nibelungen Hate*   *Joy*   *Walhall*

(Fafner) doch das Fürchten lehrt' er mich
nicht!

Arrogance   Der Welt *Erbe*
gewänne mir ein Ring!
Für der Minne Gunst
miss ich ihn gern;
ich geb ihn euch, gönnt ihr mir
    Lust.
Doch bedroht ihr mir Leben und
    Leib:
fasste er nicht
eines Fingers Wert,

Grief   den Reif entringt ihr mir *nicht*!
Ring   Denn Leben und Leib,
seht: – so –
werf ich sie weit von mir!

ALLE DREI
Kommt, Schwestern!
Schwindet dem Toren!
So weise und stark
verwähnt sich der Held,
als gebunden und blind er doch ist.
Eide schwur er –
und achtet sie nicht!
Runen weiss er –
und rät sie nicht!

FLOSSHILDE und WOGLINDE

Brünnhilde   Ein *hehr*stes Gut
ward ihm gegönnt.

DIE DREI
Dass er's verworfen,
weiss er nicht.

FLOSSHILDE
Nur den Ring –

WELLGUNDE
– der zum Tod ihm taugt –

ALLE DREI

Ring   – den Reif nur will er sich *wahr*en!
Leb wohl, Siegfried!
Ein stolzes Weib
wird noch heut dich Argen beerben.

but he could not harrow my heart.

The world's wealth
would be his who owns this ring:
yet one word of love
wins it from me.
I'd leave it to you, just for
  love;
but you threaten my life and my
  limbs:
now, were it less
than a finger's worth,
you shall not ransom the ring!
My life and my limbs,
see! – thus,
I let them go with the wind!
[he picks up a clod of earth and throws it
over his shoulder]

Sixteenth-century mercenaries
threw a clump of earth over their
shoulder before going into battle:
a symbolic gesture, denoting their
dissociation from the world.

Mythological man preferred death
to a life of fear. So does Siegfried.

ALL THREE
Come, sisters!
Leave the dumb hero!
So sane and so sound
he fancies himself,
but in bonds is this hero and blind.
Oaths he swears
and forswears his oaths!
Runes he knows
and rejects the runes!

FLOSSHILDE and WOGLINDE
The greatest boon
was granted him –

ALL THREE
– and he disowned it,
unawares.

FLOSSHILDE
Yet the ring –

WELLGUNDE
– the accursed ring –

ALL THREE
– that ring he will not surrender!
Farewell, Siegfried!
A noble wife
will today inherit your treasure.

(Ring) Sie beut uns bessres Gehör.
Zu ihr! Zu ihr! Zu ihr!

Weialala, weialala …

SIEGFRIED
Im Wasser wie am Lande
lernte nun ich Weiberart:
wer nicht ihrem Schmeicheln
    traut,
den schrecken sie mit Drohen;
wer dem kühnlich trotzt,
dem kommt dann ihr Keifen dran.
Und doch,
trüg ich nicht Gutrun Treu,
der zieren Frauen eine
hätt ich mir frisch gezähmt!

She is more lavish than you.
To her! To her! To her!
[They resume their swimming, and
gradually disappear. Siegfried looks after
them, first smiling, then meditating.]
Weialala, weialala …

SIEGFRIED
I learnt, on land and water,
women's wiles and women's ways:
when fawning and flattery
   fails,
they try to make us tremble,
and if we say no,
they sting us with scolding tongue.
And yet,
were I not Gutrun's man,
a pretty little mermaid
would be my pet by now.

As they swim away, the Rhinemaidens' departure is illustrated
by four harps which are answered
by two off-stage harps, thus
reversing the process at the
beginning of the scene.

At the beginning of *Rheingold* the
Rhinemaidens rejected Alberich,
who then stole their gold. Now
Siegfried rejects the Rhinemaidens, and keeps Alberich's
golden ring.

III. Akt: 2. Szene

HAGENS STIMME
Hoiho!

MANNEN
Hoiho! Hoiho!

SIEGFRIED
*Hoi*ho! Hoiho! Hoihe!

HAGEN
Finden wir endlich,
wohin du flogest?

SIEGFRIED
Kommt herab! Hier ist's frisch und
    kühl!

HAGEN
Hier rasten wir
und rüsten das Mahl.
Lasst ruhn die Beute
und bietet die Schläuche!
Der uns das Wild verscheuchte,
nun sollt ihr Wunder hören,
was Siegfried sich erjagt.

SIEGFRIED
Schlimm steht es um mein Mahl:
von eurer Beute
bitte ich für mich.

HAGEN
Du beutelos?

SIEGFRIED
Auf Wald*jagd* zog ich aus,
doch Wasserwild zeigte sich nur.
War ich *dazu* recht beraten,

Act III: Scene 2

HAGEN'S VOICE [from afar]
Hoiho!
[Hunting horns in the distance. Siegfried
answers their call with his.]

VASSALS
Hoiho! Hoiho!

SIEGFRIED
Hoiho! Hoiho! Hoihe!

HAGEN [appears, followed by Gunther]
Now we have found you.
You flew before us!

SIEGFRIED
Come down here! See, it's fresh
   and cool!

HAGEN
Here rest we now.
Make ready our meal!
Put down the booty,
and pass round the wineskins.
You charmed away our quarry:
pay heed now to the tidings
of Siegfried and his chase!

SIEGFRIED
No game I gained today:
so I must beg
for morsels from your meal.

HAGEN
No game at all?

SIEGFRIED
For wood-game I set out,
but water-fowl found I alone.
If I were a fishing fellow,

To the Gutrune motif (the
inverted Horn Call), the fiendish
Gibichungs summon Siegfried to
his place of execution. Gutrune is
his angel of death.

The first syllable of 'Hoihe' is a
high C. 'Today I have given
Siegfried a veritable scream. The
fellow shrieks like a wild goose.'
(Cosima's diaries, 25 February
1872) In fact, Siegfried's three
calls are sung to the Hagen motif.
Do they denote his unconscious
death-wish?

Hagen demonstrates himself a
fiendishly skilled guide to
Siegfried's doom. The answers he
elicits from his victim must
appear, to all witnesses, as a con-
fession of his great guilt.

(Horn Call) drei wilde Wasservögel
hätt ich euch wohl gefangen,
die dort auf dem Rhein mir
    sangen,

Grief   *Revenge* *er*schlagen würd ich noch *heut.*

HAGEN
Das wäre üble Jagd,
wenn den Beutelosen selbst
ein lauernd Wild erlegte!

SIEGFRIED
Mich dürstet!

HAGEN
Ich hörte sagen, Siegfried,
Woodbird der Vögel *Sanges*sprache
verstündest du wohl.
So wäre das wahr?

SIEGFRIED
Seit lange acht ich
Gutrune des Lallens nicht mehr.
Trink, Gunther, trink!
Dein Bruder bringt es dir!

GUNTHER
Atonement   *Consorts* Du mischtest matt und bleich;
Grief *dein* Blut allein darin!

SIEGFRIED

Loge + Gutrune So misch es mit dem *dei*nen!
Nun floss gemischt es über:
der Mutter Erde
Loge lass *das* ein Labsal sein!

GUNTHER
Du überfroher Held!

SIEGFRIED
Tarnhelm Ihm *macht* Brünnhilde Müh?

HAGEN
Verstünd er sie so gut,
wie du der Vöglein Sang!

a brood of water birds
would I have won as booty.
They sang from the Rhine that
  Siegfried
today was doomed to be slain.
[He sits down between Gunther and Hagen.
Gunther shudders.]

HAGEN
It were a fiendish chase,
if the luckless hunter fell,
laid low by his own quarry!

SIEGFRIED
I'm thirsty!

HAGEN [offers Siegfried a drinking-horn]
It has been whispered, Siegfried,
that when the birds are singing,
you know *what* they say:
how could that be true?

SIEGFRIED
I hardly heed
what they chatter and chirp.
Drink, Gunther, drink!
Your brother drinks to you!
[he offers the horn to Gunther]

GUNTHER
This drink is dull and dead:
Not wine I see, but blood.

SIEGFRIED [mixes his wine with
Gunther's]
Let yours and mine be mingled!
The cups are overflowing:
to earth, our mother,
a cordial it shall be!

GUNTHER [with a deep sigh]
You over-joyous heart!

SIEGFRIED [to Hagen]
He sighs Brünnhilde's sighs?

HAGEN
She does not speak to him,
as speak the birds to you!

Hagen's ghoulish jest

A sequel to the earlier Bloodbrotherhood scene

		SIEGFRIED
	Woodbird	Seit Frau*en* ich singen hörte,
		vergass ich der Vöglein ganz.

HAGEN
Doch einst vernahmst du sie?

SIEGFRIED
Hei, Gunther,
grämlicher Mann!
Dankst du es mir,
so sing ich dir Mären

Forge aus meinen jungen *Ta*gen.

		GUNTHER
Forge	*Woodbird*	Die hör ich gern.

		HAGEN
	Forge	So singe, Held!

SIEGFRIED
Mime hiess
ein mürrischer Zwerg:
in des Neides Zwang
zog er mich auf,
dass einst das Kind,
wann kühn es erwuchs,

Dragon einen *Wurm* ihm fällt' im
Wald,

Forge der faul dort hütet einen *Hort*.
Er lehrte mich schmieden
und Erze schmelzen;
doch was der Künstler
selber nicht konnt',
des Lehrlings Mute
musst' es gelingen:
eines zerschlagnen Stahles
Stücke

Sword neu zu schweissen *zum* Schwert.
Nothung Des *Va*ters Wehr
fügt ich mir neu:

Nothung *na*gelfest
Brooding schuf ich mir *No*thung.
Tüchtig zum Kampf

Dragon dünkt' er dem Zwerg;
der führte mich nun zum Wald;
dort fällt ich Fafner, den Wurm.
Jetzt aber merkt

SIEGFRIED
I listen to songs of women,
and hushed are the songs of birds.

HAGEN
But once you heard them well?

SIEGFRIED
Hei! Gunther,
gloom-ridden man!
Give the command,
and I shall amuse you
with stories from my springtime.

GUNTHER
With all my heart. [all lie stretched out
around Siegfried who alone sits upright]

HAGEN
Sing, hero, sing!

SIEGFRIED
Mime was
a surly old dwarf.
For his profit
he sharpened my wits,
that grown to strength,
courageous and fierce,
I should kill for him Fafner, the
    fiend,
who slept, a dragon, on his hoard.
Through Mime I mastered
my smithying and smelting;
but what the teacher
failed to perform,
his bold apprentice
brought to pass:
for out of a shattered weapon's
    splinters
I created my sword.
My father's sword
fashioned anew:
hard as nails,
such now was Nothung,
fit for the fight
deemed by the dwarf.
Together we went to the woods –
there perished Fafner, the fiend.
Hear, and attend

It is not pride but naivety that
precedes Siegfried's fall.

Siegfried's narration serves two
purposes: dramatic development
and recapitulation of previous
events.

Wälsung Ordeal	wohl auf die Mär:
	Wunder muss ich euch melden.
	Von des Wurmes Blut
	mir brannten die Finger;
Wälsung Ordeal	sie *führt'* ich kühlend zum Mund:
	kaum netzt' ein wenig
	die Zunge das Nass,
	was da ein Vöglein sang,
	das konnt' ich flugs verstehn.
	Auf den Ästen sass es und sang:
Woodbird	'Hei! Siegfried gehört nun
	der Niblungen Hort!
	O fänd in der Höhle
	den Hort er jetzt!
	Wollt er den Tarnhelm gewinnen,
	der taugt' ihm zu wonniger Tat!
	Doch möcht' er den Ring sich
	erraten,
	der macht' ihn zum Walter der
	Welt!'

HAGEN
Ring und Tarnhelm
trugst du nun fort?

EINE MANNE
Wälsung Ordeal Das Vöglein hörtest du *wie*der?

SIEGFRIED
Ring und Tarnhelm
hatt ich gerafft:
da lauscht' ich wieder
dem wonnigen Laller;
der sass im Wipfel und sang:
Woodbird 'Hei!, Siegfried gehört nun
der Helm und der Ring.
O traute er Mime,
dem Treulosen, nicht!
Ihm sollt' er den Hort nur
erheben;
nun lauert er listig am Weg:

nach dem Leben trachtet er
Siegfried.
Wälsung Ordeal O traute Siegfried nicht *Mi*me!'

HAGEN
Wälsung Ordeal Es mahnte dich gut?

well to my tale:
wonders have I to tell you.
When the dragon's blood
had blistered my fingers,
I licked them cool with my lips.
The blood had scarcely
been touched by my tongue,
when birds began to warble,
and I could grasp their words.
On a bough one settled and sang:
'Hei! Siegfried inherits
the Niblungen hoard!
O, close in that cavern
the hoard is hid!
There lies the Tarnhelm in waiting,
to guide him to wonderful tasks!
But if he lays hands on the
   ring,
he will rule as the lord of the
   world!'

HAGEN
Ring and Tarnhelm
were your reward?

A VASSAL
The bird, what else did it tell you?

SIEGFRIED
Ring and Tarnhelm
I took with me.
Then once again
spoke the wonderful warbler.
It sat above me and sang:
'Hei, Siegfried inherits
the helm and the ring.
O, do not trust Mime,
the treacherous troll!
He wants to abscond with the
   treasure,
and lurks now and spies for his
   spoils.
O, he means to murder you,
   Siegfried!
Be careful, Siegfried, of Mime!'

HAGEN
It counselled you well?

This repeats the birdsong music
of the second act of *Siegfried*.
There, the Woodbird ushered
Siegfried to Brünnhilde. Here,
Hagen ushers Siegfried to his
death.

VIER MANNEN
Vergaltest du Mime?

SIEGFRIED
Mit tödlichem Tranke
trat er zu mir;
bang und stotternd
gestand er mir Böses:

Forge Nothung streckte den *Strolch*!

HAGEN
Was nicht er geschmiedet,
schmeckte doch Mime!

ZWEI MANNEN
Was wies das Vöglein dich wieder?

HAGEN

Trink erst, Held,
aus meinem Horn:
ich würzte dir holden Trank,
die Erinnerung hell dir zu

Tarnhelm *we*cken,

Amnesia *Consorts* dass Fernes nicht dir ent*fal*le!
Wälsung Ordeal *Brünnhilde*

SIEGFRIED
In Leid zu dem Wipfel
lauscht' ich hinauf;
da sass es noch und sang:

Woodbird '*Hei*, Siegfried erschlug nun
den schlimmen Zwerg!
Jetzt wüsst ich ihm noch
das herrlichste Weib.
Auf hohem Felsen sie schläft,
Feuer umbrennt ihren Saal;
durchschritt' er die Brunst,
weckt' er die Braut,
Brünnhilde wäre dann sein!'

HAGEN
Und folgtest du
Woodbird des Vögleins Rate?

FOUR VASSALS
What happened to Mime?

SIEGFRIED
A murderous drink
he offered to me,
pale and shy,
but his tongue told his falsehood.
Nothung paid him his due!

HAGEN
No good as a teacher –
farewell the creature!
[he laughs coarsely]

TWO VASSALS
What further warbled the wood
bird?

HAGEN [squeezes the juice of a herb into a
drinking-horn]
Drink, my hero,
from this horn!
I poured you a spicy drink:
through its magic you now will
remember,
what happened then and
thereafter.

SIEGFRIED [drinks]
Alone, to the bird
I listened again;
it sat aloft and sang:
'Hei! Siegfried has slain
the deceitful dwarf!
Hei! Now let him find
his heaven-born bride!
On soaring mountain she sleeps;
fire encircles the fell.
Now fare through the flames,
waken the maid:
Brünnhilde shall be your bride!'

HAGEN
And did you take
the warbler's counsel?

Hagen's potion of remembrance
is meant as antidote to his potion
of forgetfulness. This echoes the
reversal of an earlier spell:
Wotan's kiss which sent Brünnhilde to sleep, and Siegfried's kiss
which awakened her.

In the earlier *Siegfrieds Tod* there
was no memory potion, but Wagner's stage directions were
superb: 'Siegfried's memory
returns under Hagen's skilfully
targeted questioning.'

SIEGFRIED

Magic Fire | Rasch ohne Zögern
zog ich nun aus,
bis den feurigen Fels ich traf:

Freia
Sanctuary | die Lohe durchschritt ich
und fand zum Lohn
schlafend – ein wonniges Weib
in lichter Waffen Gewand.
Den Helm löst ich
der herrlichen Maid;
mein Kuss erweckte sie kühn:
Bequest | *oh, wie* mich brünstig da umschlang
der schönen Brünnhilde Arm!

GUNTHER
Hagen | Was hör ich?

HAGEN
Curse | Errätst du auch
dieser Raben Geraun?

Hagen | *Siegfried* | *R*ache rieten sie mir!

VIER MANNEN
Hagen, was tust du?

ZWEI ANDEREN
Fate | *Atonement* | Was tatest du?

GUNTHER
Atonement | Hagen, was tatest du?

HAGEN
Atonement | *Fate* | Meineid rächt' ich!
Crisis | *Fate*
Crisis

Revival | SIEGFRIED

Brünnhilde,

SIEGFRIED
Yes, without pause
I sped on my way,
till I came to the flame-girt fell.
[Gunther listens with growing amazement]
I fought through the fire
and I found the prize –
sleeping – my glorious bride,
in suit of mirror-like mail.
The maid's helmet
I took from her head.
My kiss rekindled her life.
Ah, for that fervent, fond embrace –
that day was Brünnhild my bride!

GUNTHER [springing up in horror]
What says he?
[two ravens circle over Siegfried, then
fly off]

HAGEN
What rumour
do those two ravens report?
[Siegfried, his back to Hagen, looks up]

Vengeance! Vengeance, they cry!
[He thrusts his spear into Siegfried's back.
Gunther tries to prevent him, but is too late.
Siegfried tries to crush Hagen with his
shield, but falls to the ground.]

The ravens are Wotan's spy satellites. They cannot avert Siegfried's death, they can only transmit their recorded information. Their names, according to the Edda, are Hugin (thought) and Munin (memory).

On the last note of the Siegfried motif, violins, violas and cellos tumble down in sympathy with the fallen hero.

FOUR VASSALS
Hagen! O horror!

TWO VASSALS
What have you done?

GUNTHER
Hagen, what have you done?

HAGEN
Death to traitors!
[He walks calmly away and disappears.
Gunther, grief-stricken, bends down over
Siegfried.]

SIEGFRIED
[opens his eyes, supported by two vassals]
Brünnhilde!

The Revival music with its soaring harps echoes the awakening of Brünnhilde in the third act of *Siegfried*.

		heilige Braut!
(Revival)		
	Fate	Wach auf! Öffne dein Auge!
		Wer verschloss dich
	Fate	*wie*der in Schlaf?
		Wer band dich in Schlummer so
		bang?
Siegfried		Der Wecker kam;
		er küsst dich wach,
		und aber – der Braut
		bricht er die Bande:
	Hosanna	da lacht ihm Brünnhildes Lust!
		Ach, dieses Auge,
		ewig nun offen!
		Ach, dieses Atems
Jubilation		wonniges *We*hen!
		Süsses Vergehen,
		seliges Grauen
Hagen	*Fate*	*Brünn*hild *bie*tet mir – Gruss!

Crisis	Wälsung Ordeal	Crisis	Wälsung Ordeal
Crisis	Wälsungen	Wälsung Ordeal	Sieglinde
Liebesnot	Wälsung Ordeal	Sword	Siegfried
		Hero	Brünnhilde

Heavenly bride!
Awake! Look at your lover!
Who again
has locked you in sleep?
Who bound you in slumberous
   bonds?
Your lover came,
to wake your lips,
to free you again,
tearing your fetters:
his life is Brünnhilde's love!
Ah, but those eyes,
now open for ever!
Ah, but her breathing,
tranquil and tender!
Sweetest surrender!
Blissfully dying!
Brünnhild beckons me – now!
[He falls back and dies. It is night. At
Gunther's command the vassals raise
Siegfried's body and carry it in a solemn
procession over the height.]

In the *Nibelungenlied* Siegfried's
dying thoughts are of revenge.
Wagner's Siegfried is mindful only
of Brünnhilde.

He can no longer utter coherent
sentences, only exclamations.

Siegfried's death parallels that of
his father Siegmund (*Walküre*, Act
II): arrival at a fatal rendez-vous –
period of rest – death-prophecy
ignored – death by spear-thrust.

In Wagner's prose draft to
Siegfrieds Tod (October 1848)
Siegfried's last words are:
'Brünnhild! Brünnhild! Wotan's
radiant child! How bright and lustrous you are, as you come to
meet me. You are saddling your
horse, smiling with godlike
authority, riding through the dewy
air, for here is a man fit for your
choosing. Take me now to Walhall, me whom you once had
chosen to be your spouse. There I
will drink Wotan's mead, in honour of all those heroes, the drink
which you, my radiant wish-
maiden, shall serve me.
Brünnhild! Brünnhild! Take this
my greeting!'

Siegfried's Funeral Music

Wotan's final attempt to create a workable world order through his grandson has failed. The Funeral Music celebrates the life of the hero, Siegfried, but also, more significantly, his potential achievements.

Wagner gives detailed stage directions for Siegfried's death and funeral procession: 'Siegfried sinks back and dies. All stand around him in silent sorrow ... Night has fallen. At Gunther's silent command the vassals raise Siegfried's body on his shield and carry it in solemn procession away over the cliff top. Gunther leads the procession ... The moon breaks through the clouds ... Mists rise from the Rhine, gradually hiding the procession from view.'

(Die Nacht ist hereingebrochen. Auf die stumme Ermahnung Gunther's erheben Mannen Siegfried's
(Night has come. At Gunther's mute command the Vassals raise Siegfried's corpse and during the

Leiche, und geleiten sie, mit dem Folgenden, in feierlichem Zuge über dir Felsenhöhe langsam
following, carry it away in a solemn procession over the height.)

von dannen.)

(Der Mond bricht durch die
(The moon breaks through the
espressivo

Wolken, und beleuchtet immer heller den die Berghöhe erreichenden Trauerzug.)
clouds and lights up the funeral procession more and more brightly as it reaches the height.)

SIEGLINDE
molto espress.

(Aus dem
(Mists have

Rheine sind Nebel aufgestiegen, und erfüllen allmählich die ganze Bühne, auf welcher
arisen from the Rhein and gradually fill the whole stage, where the funeral procession

der Trauerzug bereits unsichtbar geworden ist, so dass diese, während des Zwischenspieles,
has become invisible: they come quite to the front, so that the whole stage remains hidden during

gänzlich verhüllt bleibt.)
the musical interlude.)

As the heroic music subsides the mists clear; the procession has arrived at the Hall of the Gibichungs.

III. Akt: 3. Szene

GUTRUNE

Grief + Horn Call War das sein *Horn*?

Gold's Dominion Nein!
Noch kehrt er nicht heim.
Horn Call Schlimme *Träu*me
störten mir den Schlaf!
Ride Wild wieherte sein R*oss*;
Lachen Brünnhildes
weckte mich auf.
Gold's Dominion Wer war das *Weib*,
Joy   *Brünnhilde* das ich zum Ufer schreiten sah?
Fate Ich fürchte Brünnhild!
Ist sie daheim?
Hagen *Brünn*hild! Brünnhild!
Bist du wach?

Grief Leer das Gemach.
So war es sie,
Gold's Dominion die ich zum *Rhei*ne schreiten sah!
War das sein Horn?
Nein!
Gutrune + Revenge Öd alles!
Säh ich Siegfried nur bald!

HAGENS STIMME

Grief   *Revenge* *Hoi*ho! Hoiho!
Wacht auf! Wacht auf!
Lichte! Lichte!
Helle Brände!
Jagdbeute
bringen wir heim.
Grief *Hoi*ho! Hoiho!
Auf, Gutrun!
Begrüsse Siegfried!
Hero Der starke *Held*,
Revenge er kehret *heim*!

Act III: Scene 3

[The Hall of the Gibichungs. Night.]

GUTRUNE
Was that his horn?
[she listens]
No!
He has not come back.
Dreams of mischief
drove me from my bed.
How wildly neighed his horse!
How did Brünnhilde
laugh out aloud!
I thought I saw
a woman go down to the shore.
This awesome Brünnhild!
Is she within?
Brünnhild! Brünnhild!
Are you there? [she opens the door timidly]
Bare is her room.
So it was she
I saw there by the river bank!
Was that his horn?
No!
All silent!
Would that Siegfried came home!
[She is about to go to her room, when she hears Hagen's voice. Now she stands still, anxiously.]

HAGEN'S VOICE
Hoiho! Hoiho!
Awake! Awake!
Torches! Torches!
Bring bright torches!
Prize booty!
Home is the hunt!
Hoiho! Hoiho! [he enters the hall]
Up, Gutrun,
and welcome Siegfried!
The conquering hero,
here he comes!

In the *Volsunga Saga* Gudrun (Gutrune) asks Brynhild to interpret a troublesome dream.

'Brynhild laughed when she heard Gudrun sobbing.' (*Volsunga Saga*)

To the relentlessly repeated Revenge motif (bassoons, cellos and double basses), Hagen displays his own brand of ruthless ferocity.

'This is no funeral procession,' said Wagner (according to Heinrich Porges), 'but a gruesome ritual.'

GUTRUNE

Revenge Was geschah, Hagen?
Horn Call Nicht hört ich sein Horn!

HAGEN

Atonement Der *blei*che Held,
nicht bläst er es mehr;
nicht stürmt er zur Jagd,
zum Streite nicht mehr,
Liebe-Tragik *Hagen + Horn Call* noch *wirbt* er um wonnige *Frauen*.

GUTRUNE

Siegfried Was bringen die?
Grief

HAGEN

Grief Eines wilden *E*bers Beute:
Hagen *Sieg*fried, deinen toten Mann.
Fate

GUNTHER

Hagen *Gu*trun, holde Schwester,
hebe dein Auge,
schweige mir nicht!

Crisis **GUTRUNE**
Hagen *Hagen* *Sieg*fried – Siegfried er*schla*gen!
Fort, treuloser Bruder,
du Mörder meines Mannes!
O Hilfe, Hilfe!
Wehe! Wehe!
Hagen *Hagen* Sie haben *Sieg*fried er*schla*gen!

GUNTHER

Hagen Nicht klage wider mich!
Dort klage wider *Ha*gen:
Horn Call er ist der verfluchte *E*ber,
der diesen Edlen zerfleischt'.

HAGEN

Hagen Bist du mir *gram* darum?

Murder **GUNTHER**
Hagen Angst und *Un*heil
greife dich immer!

GUTRUNE [terrified]
Where is he, Hagen?
No sound from his horn?

HAGEN
This bloodless man
will blow it no more!
No more will he chase,
no more will he charge,
nor lavish more love on more
    ladies.

GUTRUNE
Whose pall is this? [the procession has
reached the centre of the hall, where the
vassals set down the body]

HAGEN
A ferocious boar has bled him.
Siegfried, your own consort – dead!
[Gutrune shrieks and falls on the body]

GUNTHER
Gutrun, sweetest sister,
do not avoid me,
speak but one word!

GUTRUNE
Siegfried! Siegfried lies murdered!
Hence, base-hearted brother!
You butchered my own husband!
O help me, help me!
Horror! Horror!
My hero, Siegfried, lies murdered!

GUNTHER
Call down no curse on me!
Call down your curse on Hagen!
He is the accursed boar
who has savaged Siegfried to
    death.

HAGEN
And you disown the deed?

GUNTHER
Harm and fear
shall haunt you forever!

Högni (Hagen): 'A wild boar dealt
him this death wound.' Grimhild
(Gutrune): 'You are that boar, and
no one else!' (*Thidrek Saga*)

In the *Nibelungenlied* Siegfried's
wounds begin to bleed as Hagen
approaches the corpse. Gunther
lies, 'Robbers have killed him.'
Kriemhild answers, 'I know those
robbers well.'

		HAGEN
Hagen	*Hagen*	*Ja* denn, ich hab ihn erschlagen.
		Ich, Hagen,
	Atonement	schlug ihn zu *Tod*.
		Meinem Speer war er gespart,
		bei dem er Meineid sprach.
		Heiliges Beuterecht
		hab ich mir nun errungen:
	Ring	drum fordr' ich hier diesen *Ring*.

GUNTHER
Zurück! Was mir verfiel,

Ring sollst nimmer du em*pfahn*.

HAGEN

Ring Ihr Mannen, richtet mein Recht!

GUNTHER

Ring *Gutrune* Rührst du an Gutrunes *Er*be,

Curse schamloser Albensohn?

HAGEN
Des Alben Erbe

Ring fordert so sein *Sohn*!
Grief
Gold's Dominion Her den *Ring*!
Sword
Götterdämmerung

BRÜNNHILDE

Genesis Schweigt eures Jammers

Götterdämmerung *Genesis* jauchzenden *Schwall*.

  Das ihr alle ver*rie*tet,

Fate zur Rache *schrei*tet sein Weib.

  Kinder hört ich

  greinen nach der Mutter,

Fate da süsse Milch sie verschüttet:

Crisis doch nicht er*klang mir*

Death würdige *Klage*,

  des hehrsten Helden wert.

GUTRUNE
Brünnhilde! Neiderboste!
Du brachtest uns diese Not:

HAGEN [with terrible defiance]
Truly! I swear that I slew him.
I, Hagen,
smote him to death.
He was forfeit to the spear
on which he was foresworn.
Mine is the hunter's due.
Do not deny the booty:
I claim my right to the ring!

GUNTHER
Stand back! It is my own.
This forfeit falls to me!

HAGEN
You vassals, side with me now!

GUNTHER
Sacred is Gutrun's dower,
infamous Niblung son!

HAGEN [drawing his sword]
My father's dower
comes now to his son!
[he fights with Gunther and kills him]
Mine the ring!
[He attempts to take the ring, when
Siegfried's hand rises menacingly. All cry
out in fear, while Brünnhilde advances
solemnly to the front.]

BRÜNNHILDE
Silence your cries
and clamour of woe!
Everyone has betrayed me;
now rightful vengeance be mine!
I see children,
mewling for their mother,
because sweet milk has spilled
    over,
but hear no words
of worthy lament
that may fit a hero's fate.

GUTRUNE
Brünnhilde, black with envy,
you brought this harm to our
    house.

'This is a replay of the fight
between the giants in *Rheingold*.'
(Wagner, according to Felix Mottl)

'Her den Ring!' ('Mine the ring!'):
Wotan used this very phrase
when he demanded Alberich's
ring in *Rheingold*. The god's mis-
demeanour is retrospectively
given a new, ignoble dimension.

Brünnhilde's entry is flanked by
the Götterdämmerung and Genesis motifs. Her demeanour is in
total contrast to that of the wild
avenger of the previous act. Her
music is serene, tender and pro-
found.

die du die Männer ihm
    verhetztest,
weh, dass du dem Haus genaht!

Grief

Gutrune

BRÜNNHILDE
Armselige, *schweig*!
Sein Eheweib warst du nie,
als Buhlerin

Bequest
bandest du ihn.
Sein Mannesgemahl bin ich,
der ewige Eide er schwur,

Amnesia
eh Siegfried je dich er*sah*.

GUTRUNE
Verfluchter Hagen,
dass du das Gift mir rietest,
das ihr den Gatten entrückt!

Ach, Jammer!
Gutrune
Wie jäh nun weiss ich's,
Brünnhild war die Traute,
die durch den Trank er vergass!

Crisis   *Fate*   *Crisis*
Fate   *Crisis*
Authority

BRÜNNHILDE
Authority
Starke Scheite
schichtet mir dort
am Rande des Rheins zuhauf!
Hoch und hell
Magic Fire
lodre die *Glut*,
Siegfried
die den edlen *Leib*

Götterdämmerung   *Ride*
des *hehr*sten Helden ver*zehrt*.
Magic Fire + Authority
Sein Ross führet daher,
dass mit mir dem Recken es
    folge;
Siegfried
denn des Helden heiligste
Ehre zu teilen,
Ride   *Authority*
verlangt mein eigener *Leib*.
Vollbringt Brünnhildes Wunsch!

Hosanna

Wie Sonne lauter
strahlt mir sein Licht:
der Reinste war er,
der mich verriet!
Die Gattin trügend,
treu dem Freunde,

You goaded all these men against
  him.
Woe came in when you came in.

BRÜNNHILDE
Be still, poor wretch!
You never were his true wife.
His paramour,
never his spouse!
His wife, his sworn wife am I.
The bond of our union was born,
before he looked at your face.

GUTRUNE
Accursed Hagen!
Accurst the fatal philtre
that charmed her spouse from her
  side!
Ah, sorrow!
At last I see it:
Brünnhild was his true love.
The drink, not he, broke his faith.
[Gutrune turns humbly away. Hagen
remains defiantly silent.]

At last, wisdom has come to
Gutrune.

Wagner's stage directions go
some way towards re-establishing
Gutrune's moral credibility: 'She
turns humbly away from Siegfried
and, sorrowfully, bends over Gunther's body. So she remains,
motionless, until the end.'

BRÜNNHILDE [to the vassals]
Let great logs
be piled up on high,
out there by the banks of the Rhine.
Proud and bright
kindle a blaze.
Let the brilliant flames
consume this hero of mine.
His steed bring to my side,
that we both may follow our
  master.
I must share my hero's
holiest homage:
both bodies blaze to the sky!
Obey Brünnhild's command!
[The men build a funeral pyre, women
bedeck it with flowers. Brünnhilde watches
tenderly.]
Such lustrous splendour
flames from his face:
none was so true
as he who was false.
So false to me,
so fair to friendship:

From William Morris's translation
of the *Volsunga Saga*: 'Let make
a great bale for me and for Si-
gurd, and lay betwixt us a drawn
sword, as in the days when we
twain stepped into one bed
together.'

'Treulos, treuester Freund' ('faithless, faithfullest friend'), says King
Mark of Tristan.

		von der eignen Trauten,
(Hosanna)	*Sword*	einzig ihm teuer,
		schied er sich durch sein Schwert.
		Echter als er
	Hosanna	schwur *kei*ner Eide;
		treuer als er
		hielt keiner Verträge;
	Liebesnot	*lau*trer als er
Hosanna		liebte kein *an*drer.
		Und doch, alle Eide,
Nothung		alle Verträge,
	Death	trog keiner wie er!

| *Death* | *Walhall* | Wisst ihr, wie das ward? |

O ihr, der Eide
heilige Hüter!
Lenkt euren Blick
auf mein blühendes Leid,

| *Death* | *Wotan's Child* | er*schaut* eure ewige *Schuld*! |

Meine Klage hör,

| *Fate* | *Wotan's Child* | du *hehr*ster *Gott*! |

Durch seine *tap*ferste *Tat*,
dir so tauglich erwünscht,
weihtest du den,
der sie gewirkt,
dem Fluche, dem du verfielest.
Mich musste
der Reinste verraten,

| *Fate* | *Crisis* | dass *wis*send würde ein Weib! |
| *Fate* | *Crisis* | *Weiss* ich nun, was dir frommt? |

*Al*les, alles,
alles weiss ich,

| *Grief* | alles ward mir nun frei. |

Auch deine Raben
hör ich rauschen;
mit bang ersehnter Botschaft

Curse	*Walhall*	send ich die bei*den* nun heim.
	Erda	Ruhe, *ruhe*, du Gott!
	Authority	
Götterdämmerung	*Genesis*	

Mein Erbe nun

| *Ring* | nehm ich zu *ei*gen. |

Verfluchter *Reif*!

| *Grief* | Furchtbarer *Ring*! |

Dein Gold fass ich
und geb es nun fort.

when his loving spouse
did lie by his side,
his sword kept love from his love.
No one so true,
so true to treaties.
No one so pure,
so pure in his promise.
No one like him,
lord of all loving.
Yet never was treaty,
never was promise,
and never was love
so truly betrayed.
Shall I tell you why?
[looking heavenwards]
Eternal gods,
who guard solemn pledges,
turn, turn your eyes
on my full-flowing shame:
behold your own shame in full
    flow!
Hear my heartsick moan,
you mighty god!
When Siegfried captured the ring,
you desired the deed.
Yet you would doom
him whom you loved,
and curse him as you are curséd.
I, Brünnhild,
betrayed by my lover,
but understanding it all:
what must be, let it be.
All things, all things,
all I know now,
all is clear to my eyes!
Here are your ravens:
see them hover!
With tidings feared and longed for,
let them fly home to their lord!
Rest then, rest then, o god!
[The vassals lift Siegfried's body on to the
funeral pyre. Brünnhilde draws the ring
from Siegfried's finger.]
My heritage
comes to my keeping.
Repugnant gold!
Terrible ring!
My hand holds you
and gives you away.

With the undulating fragments of
the Walhall motif Brünnhilde
rocks Wotan to sleep.

Wagner telescopes an early and a
late phrase from *Hamlet*: 'Rest,
perturbed spirit', and 'The rest is
silence.'

Innocence	Der Wassertiefe
	weise *Schwe*stern,
	des Rheines schwimmende
	Töchter,
	euch dank ich redlichen Rat.
	Was ihr begehrt,
Rhinegold	ich geb es euch:
	aus meiner Asche
	nehmt es zu eigen!
	Das Feuer, das mich verbrennt,
	reinge vom Fluche den Ring!
	Ihr in der Flut
	löset ihn auf,
	und lauter bewahrt
Ring	das lichte *Gold*,
Curse	das *euch zum* Unheil geraubt.
Fate *Treaty*	
Loge	

Magic Fire	Fliegt heim, ihr *R*aben!
	Raunt es eurem Herren,
	was hier am Rhein ihr gehört!
	An Brünnhildes Felsen
	fahrt vorbei.
	Der dort noch lodert,
Götterdämmerung	weiset Loge nach *Wal*hall!
Genesis	Denn der Götter *E*nde
Götterdämmerung	dämmert nun *auf*.
	So – werf ich den Brand
Walhall	in Walhalls prangende *Burg*.
Loge *Valkyrie Cry*	
Ride *Loge* *Ride*	

Loge *Ride*	Grane, mein Ross,
	sei mir gegrüsst!
	Weisst du auch, mein Freund,
Assurance	wohin ich dich führe?
Siegfried *Assurance*	Im Feuer *leuch*tend,
	liegt dort dein *Herr*,
Ride	Siegfried, mein seliger Held.
Valkyrie Cry *Loge*	Dem *Freun*de zu folgen,
	wieherst du freudig?
Valkyrie Cry *Magic Fire*	*Lockt* dich zu ihm
	die lachende Lohe?
Magic Fire *Assurance*	Fühl meine Brust auch,
	wie sie entbrennt;
	helles Feuer

You water-dwellers,
maids of wisdom,
the Rhine's fair, radiant
    daughters,
good counsel gave you to me.
What you would have,
you shall have now.
From Brünnhild's ashes
take it for ever!
This fire, burning my limbs,
cleanses the ring of its curse.
Down in the waves,
wash it away,
and purer preserve
your wondrous gold,
whose plunder plagued the whole
    world.

[with the ring on her finger, she turns to the
pyre and seizes a great torch from one of
the vassals]

Fly home, you ravens!
Tell your lord the tidings
that you have witnessed today.
By Brünnhilde's fell-side
wing your flight.
The rock still blazes.
Summon Loge to Walhall,
for the final dusk
descends on the gods.
Thus, hurled be this brand
at Walhall's proud-blazing
    pomp!

[She throws the brand on the pyre. Two
ravens fly up and away. She hastens
towards her horse.]

Grane, my steed,
be welcome here!
Do you know, my friend,
what course we shall follow?
In flame-girt glory
there lies your lord,
Siegfried, the star of my life.
So join your own master,
neighing your greeting,
lured by the flames,
their light and their laughter.
Now feel my breast, friend,
its fiery blaze!
Sacred fever

Brünnhilde's funeral pyre was foreshadowed in her father's order to surround Walhall with the logs of the World Ash Tree. On earth as it is in heaven.

A vital clue to the debatable meaning of the ending of the *Ring* is given as Brünnhilde predicts the demise of the gods: the word 'Ende' is sung to the Genesis motif!

To the Assurance motif, Brünnhilde had told Sieglinde of the forthcoming birth of Siegfried (*Walküre*, Act II). Now the same motif pledges the husband and wife's togetherness.

				das Herz mir erfasst,
				ihn zu umschlingen,
				umschlossen von ihm,
				in mächtigster Minne
				vermählt ihm zu sein!

(Assurance)

	Siegfried + Valkyrie Cry	*Hei*ajoho! Grane!
	Siegfried	Grüss deinen Herren!
	Assurance	Siegfried! Sie*gfried! Sieh!*
Valkyrie Cry	*Ride*	Selig grüsst dich dein Weib!

Magic Fire

Grief

Joy

HAGEN
Zurück vom Ring!

Curse	*Innocence*	*Walhall*	*Innocence*
Assurance	*Walhall*	*Innocence*	*Assurance*
	Walhall + Authority		*Siegfried*
	Götterdämmerung		
	Assurance		

lays hold of my heart –
him to embrace,
and embraced but by him –
our love is eternal –
our love, it is now!
Heiajoho! Grane,
ride we to greet him!
Siegfried! Siegfried! See!
Brünnhild brings you her life!
[She mounts her horse and makes it leap
into the fire. Flames envelop the hall. The
Rhine overflows its banks. At the appearance
of the Rhinemaidens, Hagen is seized with
alarm and rushes into the flood.]

HAGEN
The ring! My ring!
[Woglinde and Wellgunde draw him into the
depths. Flosshilde holds the regained ring,
triumphantly. Wotan and his gods and
heroes are seen, seated in Walhall, as
Waltraute had described it in Act I. The fire
seizes the hall of the gods, while the men
and women watch in great agitation.]

The curtain falls.

Shortly before the end we hear
the Walhall and Authority motifs
combined. This signifies Wotan's
final deed, which the Norns predicted: 'the demolished weapon's
transfixing splinters Wotan
plunges in Loge's smouldering
breast.'

By integrating the death of
Siegfried with that of Brünnhilde,
Wagner creates a new myth which
merges the world of gods and
men, a final meeting of myth and
history.

'I wish to become a Protestant, so
that I can be cremated and buried
with Richard.' (Cosima's diaries, 2
March 1871)

Survivors and Casualties

GODS
Wotan ⌉
Fricka │
Freia ├ all perish in the final conflagration
Froh │
Donner ⌋
Erda   possible survivor
Loge   survives

VALKYRIES
Brünnhilde perishes in the final conflagration, as do Gerhilde, Ortlinde, Waltraute, Schwertleite, Helmwige, Siegrune, Grimgerde and Rossweisse.

RHINEMAIDENS
Woglinde ⌉
Wellgunde ├ all survive
Flosshilde ⌋

GIANTS
Fafner   killed by Siegfried
Fasolt   killed by Fafner

Alberich   survives
Mime   killed by Siegfried
Siegmund   killed by Hunding
Sieglinde   dies in childbirth
Hunding   killed by Wotan
Siegfried   killed by Hagen
Gunther   killed by Hagen
Gutrune   possible survivor
Hagen   drowned by Woglinde and Wellgunde
Norns   possible survivors

Wagner's *Ring* Road

	Text	**Music**	
Siegfrieds Tod	October 1848 to December 1852	October 1869 to November 1874	↑ *Götterdämmerung*
		March 1869 to February 1871	*Siegfried* Act III
Der junge Siegfried	May 1851 to December 1852	September 1856 to August 1857	*Siegfried* Acts I and II
Walküre	November 1851 to July 1852	June 1854 to March 1856	*Walküre*
Rheingold	November 1851 to November 1852	November 1853 to September 1854	*Rheingold*

History of *Götterdämmerung*

Composition History

1848	October	Prose draft: *Siegfrieds Tod* completed
1852	December	Verse draft: *Siegfrieds Tod* completed
1869	October	Composition of *Götterdämmerung* begun
1874	November	Composition of *Götterdämmerung* completed

Performance History

1876	August	First performance (as part of *Ring* cycle): Festspielhaus, Bayreuth
1882	May	First British performance: Her Majesty's Theatre, London

Bibliography

Further Reading

A more complete bibliography is given in the author's companion volume in this series.

Bailey, R. 'Wagner's Musical Sketches for Siegfrieds Tod' in *Essays for Oliver Strunk* (Princeton, 1968)

Benvenga, N. *Kingdom on the Rhine* (Harwich, 1983)

Blyth, A. *Wagner's 'Ring'* (London, 1980)

Burbridge, P. & Sutton, R., eds. *The Wagner Companion* (London, 1979)

Cooke, D. *I Saw the World End* (London, 1979)

Dahlhaus, C. *Die Musikdramen Richard Wagners* (Velber, 1971; Eng. trans., 1979)

Donington, R. *Wagner's 'Ring' and its Symbols* (London, 1963)

English National Opera Guide: *The Twilight of the Gods* (London, 1985)

Kobbé, G. *Wagner's Ring of the Nibelung* (New York, 1897)

Lee, M. O. *Wagner's 'Ring'* (New York, 1990)

Leroy, L. A. *Wagner's Music Drama of the Ring* (London, 1925)

Magee, E. *Richard Wagner and the Nibelungs* (Oxford, 1990)

Mander R. & Mitchenson, J. *The Wagner Compendium* (London, 1977)

Millington, B., ed. *The Wagner Compendium* (London, 1992)

Newman, E. *Wagner Nights* (London, 1949)

Osborne, C. *The Complete Operas of Richard Wagner* (London, 1990)

Porges, H. *Die Bühnenproben zu den Bayreuther Festspielen des Jahres 1876* (Bayreuth, 1881–96; Eng. trans., 1983, as *Wagner Rehearsing the Ring*)

Porter, A. trans. *Richard Wagner: The Ring* (London, 1976)

Shaw, G. B. *The Perfect Wagnerite* (London, 1898, 4/1923/repr. 1972)

Skelton, G. *Wagner at Bayreuth* (London, 1976)

Spencer, S., trans. *Wagner's Ring of the Nibelung* (London, 1993)

Spotts, F. *Bayreuth, A History of the Wagner Festival* (New Haven, 1994)

Weston, J. L. *The Legends of the Wagner Dramas* (London, 1896)

Discography

Four recommended performances. An extended discography can be found in the companion volume.

1950
Wilhelm Furtwängler
La Scala Orchestra and Chorus
Siegfried: M. Lorenz
Gutrune: H. Konetzni
Brünnhilde: K. Flagstad
Waltraute: E. Höngen
Gunther: J. Hermann
Alberich: A. Pernerstorfer
Hagen: L. Weber
A historic document of great importance! Furtwängler makes his orchestra respond to the sublety of his rubatos. Max Lorenz and Kirsten Flagstad are simply overwhelming, notwithstanding the tenor's cavalier treatment of rhythmic niceties. Weber's Hagen is awe-inspiring, and there is not a weak link in this master cast. The sound is very acceptable for its age. Let us give thanks for Wilhelm Furtwängler.
CETRA CDC28 (Mono)

1964
Georg Solti
Vienna Philharmonic and State Opera Chorus
Siegfried: W. Windgassen
Brünnhilde: B. Nilsson
Gunther: D. Fischer-Dieskau
Hagen: G. Frick
Gutrune: C. Watson

Waltraute: C. Ludwig
Alberich: G. Neidlinger
An unsurpassable cast without exception offers superb interpretations and vocal brilliance. Windgassen and Nilsson are totally committed – listen to the end of Act I, with Siegfried turning into a most unwilling anti-hero, and Brünnhilde plumbing the depths of divine despair. Fischer-Dieskau and Claire Watson raise the doubtful prestige of the feeble Gibichung siblings with their mellifluous portrayals, while Christa Ludwig's Waltraute has never been bettered. Which other set can boast such Rhinemaidens as Lucia Popp and Gwyneth Jones?
DECCA 414115-2DH4

1967
Karl Böhm
Bayreuth Festival Orchestra and Chorus
Siegfried: W. Windgassen
Brünnhilde: B. Nilsson
Gunther: T. Stewart
Hagen: J. Greindl
Gutrune: L. Dvoráková
Waltraute: M. Mödl
Alberich: G. Neidlinger
Outstanding in this superb cast are, of course, Nilsson and Windgassen, but what a finely honed and burnished baritone this set can boast in Thomas Stewart's Gunther. Anja Silja's Third Norn marked, alas, her last appearance at Bayreuth and, until recently, in the Wagner repertoire. Böhm's Straussian inclinations make such passages as Siegfried's Rhine Journey a jaunty voyage rather than a trip into

disaster. This set, remarkably, features three renowned Brünnhildes in minor parts, Martha Mödl (Waltraute), Ludmilla Dvoráková (Gutrune) and Helga Dernesch (Wellgunde).
PHILIPS 412488-2PH4

1989
James Levine
Metropolitan Opera Orchestra and Chorus
Siegfried: R. Goldberg
Brünnhilde: H. Behrens
Gunther: B. Weikl
Hagen: M. Salminen
Gutrune: C. Studer
Waltraute: H. Schwarz
Alberich: E. Wlaschiha
This is a set overflowing with felicities. The New York orchestra is brilliant, and James Levine's many years in Bayreuth have made him an outstanding Wagnerian. His cast is uniformly superb. Reiner Goldberg, disliked by many critics is to my ears a strong, mellifluous Siegfried. His Brünnhilde, Hildegard Behrens, gives unsparingly of her ample resources, dramatically awesome and heart-rending in her distress. In Matti Salminen's Hagen, Cheryl Studer's Gutrune, Ekkehard Wlaschiha's Alberich and Hanna Schwarz's Waltraute we have the world's top performers in their respective roles. A great set.
DG 445354-2GX14

Videography

There are four performances of *Götterdämmerung* on video. The companion volume gives details of the other dramas in the cycle.

Place	Bayreuth	Munich	New York	Bayreuth
Orchestra	Festival	Bavarian. State	Met. Opera	Festival
Conductor	P. Boulez	W. Sawallisch	J. Levine	D. Barenboim
Producer	P. Chéreau	N. Lehnhoff	O. Schenk	H. Kupfer
Year	1980	1989	1990	1992
Video	Philips 070401/2/3/4 3PHE2	EMI MVX9 91275-3	DG 072 418/19/20/21 3GH2	Teldec 4509 91123-3
Laserdisc	070 401-4 1PHE2/3	LDX9 91275-1	072 418-21 1GH2/3/3/3	4509 91122/3-6 and 94193/4-6
SIEGFRIED	M. Jung	R. Kollo	S. Jerusalem	S. Jerusalem
BRÜNNHILDE	G. Jones	H. Behrens	H. Behrens	A. Evans
GUNTHER	F. Mazura	H. G. Nöcker	A. Raffell	B. Brinkmann
HAGEN	F. Hübner	M. Salminen	M. Salminen	P. Kang
GUTRUNE	J. Altmeyer	L. Balslev	H. Lisowska	E. Bundschuh
WALTRAUTE	G. Killebrew	W. Meier	C. Ludxig	W. Meier
ALBERICH	H. Becht	E. Wlaschiha	M. Salminen	G. von Kannen

Leitmotifs of *Götterdämmerung*

In this alphabetical list of all leitmotifs in *Götterdämmerung,* letters 'R', 'W' and 'S' are added when the motif also appeared in the preceding operas of the cycle, *Das Rheingold, Die Walküre* and *Siegfried.*

Action S

Amnesia

Arrogance R, S

Assurance W

Atonement W

Authority S

Bequest   S

Bloodbrothers

Brooding   S

Brünnhilde

Consorts

Crisis   R, W, S

Curse   R, W, S

Death   W, S

Dragon   R, W, S

Erda   R, W, S

Fafner S

pp

Fate W, S

Forge R, S

Freia R, W, S

Freedom S

SIEGFRIED

Aus dem Wald fort in die Welt ziehn: nim-mer kehr ich zu - ruck'

Genesis R, S

Gibichungen

Golden Apples R

Gold's Dominion R

Götterdämmerung R, S

Grief

Gutrune

Hagen

Hero

Horn Call
S

Hosanna
S

Innocence
R

Joy
R, S

Jubilation
S

Liebesbund
S

Liebesglück   S

(teurig, doch zart.)

O Sieg - fried, Herr - li - cher! Hort ___ der Welt!

Liebesnot   R, W, S

Liebe-Tragik   R, W, S

Loge   R, W, S

Magio Fire   W, S

Murder

Nibelungen Hate   R, W, S

Nothung   W, S

No - thung!

Oblivion   W, S

Revenge

Revival   S

Rhinegold   R, W, S

Ride   W, S

Ring   R, W, S

Sanctuary   W, S

Siegfried   W, S

Sieglinde   W, S

Sword   R, W, S

Tarnhelm   R, S

Treaty R, W, S

Walhall R, W, S

Valkyrie Cry W, S

Wälsungen W, S

Wälsung Ordeal W, S

Woodbird S

Wotan's Frustration W, S

Wotan's Child W, S

Photographic Acknowledgements

AKG London: 90
AKG London/Munich, Private Collection: 38
Bayreuther Festspiele GmbH: 18
Bayreuther Festspiele GmbH/Siegfried Lauterwasser: 94
The Lebrecht Collection: 41
Mary Evans Picture Library: 2, 142, 144
Mary Evans/Arthur Rackham Collection: 14, 17, 92, 147
National Archiv der Richard-Wagner-Stiftung, Bayreuth: 42